AF471170

# Lace in the Making

TABLIER OF PILLOW LACE: Brussels. Late 17th Cent.

(*In the Victoria and Albert Museum.*)

# Lace in the Making

## WITH BOBBINS AND NEEDLE

By
MARGARET L. BROOKE

*With Line Illustrations by*
WINIFRED M. A. BROOKE
*and Photographs of Lace in the Victoria and
Albert Museum, etc.*

Routledge & Kegan Paul
London and Henley

*First published in 1923*
*Reprinted in 1975 and 1978*
*by Routledge & Kegan Paul Ltd*
*39 Store Street*
*London WC1E 7DD and*
*Broadway House, Newtown Road*
*Henley-on-Thames*
*Oxon RG9 1EN*
*Printed in Great Britain by*
*Lowe & Brydone Printers Ltd, Thetford, Norfolk*

*ISBN 0 7100 8230 4*

# CONTENTS

# LIST OF ILLUSTRATIONS

## PLATES

# INTRODUCTION

THE present work is a handbook of directions for lace-making and in it detailed and illustrated instructions, suited both for elementary and advanced students, are given for the production of the principal kinds of Bobbin and Needle Laces.

The chief feature of the book, however, is that a considerable number of new stitches and methods are introduced by it.

In regard to Bobbin Lace :—Up to the present time there have been only two kinds of clothwork in general use, whole or linen stitch and half stitch ; while more than a dozen new kinds are given here, beside half a dozen ways of embroidering plain clothwork.

But four good edges are in ordinary employment, while in this eight fresh ones are introduced.

Two old kinds of " raised work " are recognised and four new ones are illustrated in this work.

The numbers of bars in use are seven. Four others are described here.

Old " fillings " are too numerous to be counted, but a dozen novelties are explained in this, some of which will be found very distinctive.

An account is given of the striking lace called Devonian, and of a new kind called " Skeleton Leaf " ; which is easy, quick in the making and effective. The general methods and principal stitches of Needle Lace are also carefully explained.

The writer has given a short sketch of the History and Development of Lace, with a list of Laces and their Centres, also a Glossary; and her husband has compiled a Bibliography of works on lace published in England and on the Continent during the last hundred years, which is also included. (Fig. 113.)  A Table of the development of lace between 1540 and 1881 by Mr Alan S. Cole, C.B., is, with his kind permission, likewise inserted.

# LACE IN THE MAKING

## CHAPTER I

## PILLOW LACE

**METHODS.**—The varieties of pillow lace are grouped naturally in two principal divisions, according to the methods by which they are worked.

Of these, the section which is, perhaps, most widely known and attempted, includes such styles as Torchon, Guipure, Maltese, Buckingham, and Mechlin. In this division ornament and ground are worked together by an alternation of open and close work—the close work forming the pattern and the more open part the grounding.

The second division comprises the laces called Brussels, Honiton, Bruges, and Russian, with some less-known types from the Vosges and some countries in the North of Europe. The characteristic feature of these varieties is that the pattern, with its flowers, scrolls, and footing, is made first, and the ground, of bars or nets put in afterwards, with separate bobbins. Even so small a space as the centre of a flower would probably be treated in this manner.

The second method is the easier and simpler to learn and, having mastered it, an intelligent student can find out for herself how to make the other varieties with the help of a piece of lace and a magnifying-glass.

While, in making any given variety, the general methods of English and Belgian workers are much alike, they differ considerably in some of their minor details.

We must, I think, acknowledge the Belgians to be the more perfect craftswomen, and this not so much that they do better work, but they follow many generations of well-attested traditions and have confidence in themselves as recognised masters of their craft. They have left the days of amateurism far behind them.

A good example of the difference between Honiton and Brussels methods, both of designing and working, may be seen in their respective treatment of a conventional rose—formed, in both countries, by an inner circle of braid continued for another revolution in waves more or less accentuated.

In Brussels, the designer of such an ornament generally makes the inner circle very narrow and the worker follows the idea, although, to save trouble, she uses as many bobbins as this aim will permit.

In Honiton designer and worker will often aim only at a circle of ordinary width.

In the outer circle, the Brussels designer accentuates the waves and applies them with more or less flat turns to the edge of the centre circle, giving the idea of petals round a central cup.

The Honiton designer arranges for a braid of even width for the outer circle, with waves rounded both towards the centre and circumference ; while the worker strives more for good work after the tradition of her forerunners than to make certain whether the result shall more resemble a blossom or a berry.  So long as it is a well-made sprig the ideal is fulfilled.

The foregoing, of course, applies only to the generality of workers in both countries.  The work of an expert knows no rule.

Pillow lace appears to have advanced less in modern years than most other kinds of handicraft ; probably owing to the unusual character of the appliances by means of which it is made.  Yet the bobbins, pillow and pins, form practically nothing more than a small loom.   Let the expert sweep aside the cramping fetters of tradition and use this loom, as she uses her needle and thread, to work out the fancies of a fertile brain, and mankind will have lace of novel, as well as beautiful, texture to admire. Woman as an inventor is no longer remarkable.

The class of persons to whom pillow lace should be the greatest boon, is that comprising educated invalids.  Its varying degrees of difficulty, its many openings for artistic talent, both in designing and working, and the easy way in which the work is uncovered for use and put up again, combine to make it an ideal occupation for those who need an absorbing employment, and yet are easily fatigued.

**Designs.**—The want of originality and grace in its designs was a very serious cause of that decline of English lace which took place in the latter half of the nineteenth century.

The patterns used were mostly old and had been, for generations of workers, slavishly copied pinhole by pinhole.  Slavishly —but not always exactly.  Mistakes, from time to time, would occur, and these were copied with further slips till very quaint results were obtained.  The original meaning of many old patterns can only be guessed : so that restoration is most difficult.

The very idea of designing frightens many people : yet, if the methods of lace making be well known, it is not difficult to make a simple lace pattern. It is worth while to try for oneself, even if the pattern produced be not so pretty as a bought one. It will, at least, be fresh, which is always an attraction ; while a little practice, with the study of some manual on designing, will often be sufficient for the production of a pattern which will give value to one's work, especially to that intended for a present.

In preparing a design, correctness of detail is most important so that nothing should be left to the judgment of the eye that square-ruled paper, compasses, and ruler can deal with more exactly.

As for subjects for lace designs, the field is wide from which to gather them. Leaves from the roadside, flowers from nature, books, or even wall-paper, conventional designs from the stone or iron work of old churches or other buildings, with many things among the ordinary surroundings of daily life, may give the first idea of a really good pattern.

Shells and seaweeds work into flowing designs of great beauty. Orchids are rather difficult to delineate, but give distinction and are certainly not hackneyed. A good effect too in skilful hands should be obtained by petals dropped with apparent carelessness on net.

In designing, strength and close connection should be given to the entire edge ; while strong union should be maintained, at frequent intervals, between the footing and the upper edge. It is neglect of one or other of these two points that is so often the cause of rents in good old lace.

In patterns intended to be used for work which is to be sold, it is important to study fashion. Peculiar shapes, and such as show date quickly, are better avoided ; while intelligent consideration will gather the trend of the coming styles, and shapes can be chosen that are fashionable at the time of making and still, by easy changes, may keep the air of being in the newest mode for seasons yet to come.

Some things, such as handkerchiefs, borders, and berthas, are always worn : but even with these it is possible to produce patterns that seem familiar to every beholder, and equally practicable, with a little consideration, to arrange something of an appearance new and striking.

CHAPTER II

# OUTFIT

**REQUISITES.**—As an equipment for the manufacture of pillow lace, the worker will need :—

A pillow, whereon the pattern may be fixed, with a stand on which to support it.

Patterns, on which perforations show the correct places for the supporting pins.

Thread, of which the lace is made.

Bobbins, on which that thread is wound, for convenience in working and a case in which to keep them.

Pins, to keep the thread in place while the lace is being made.

A pincushion, about 4 in. square, provided with a loop of ribbon, by which it may be pinned upon the pillow.

A needle-pin, tractor, or calyx-eyed needle, for uniting the various parts of the pattern.

Also carrying cases to hold pillows and accessories.

The writer has found leaf-stitch pins useful, and a bobbin-winder is certainly a great time-saver.

**Pillows and How to Make Them.**—Pillows, which are used in the manufacture of the various kinds of lace, differ considerably for very apparent reasons.

They vary in different provinces, from the same reason that dialects are diverse, they have developed from different sources, and among unlike surroundings and circumstances. They also differ with the method of working.

The lace made in the Midlands is generally worked backwards and forwards across the pillow, from one side to the other, in parallel or diagonal lines : in what might be called an endless strip. For this, the sofa bolster shape is found convenient, with the addition of a large, square pillow for making handkerchiefs, collars, etc.

In Brussels and Honiton lace, each warp or lengthwise thread lies approximately parallel with the edge of that part of the work which it helps to make. Thus, as the stem or blossom curves, the bobbins must hang in turn over every part of the pillow. In making a circular flower, they would hang at first over the front, next over the right end, then over the back and finally over the left. That is, the position in regard to the worker would be so if she did not turn the pillow; though, naturally, as a matter of practice, the pillow would always be placed so that the bobbins were in front of the worker.

For this lace, when made in narrow borders, the usual and convenient shape is a shortened sofa bolster with its diameter from end to end little greater than that of its thickness. Patterns can be placed round it, one after another, to whatever length may be necessary: and bobbins will keep any position required of them with tolerable amiability; whereas if the pillow is much longer than its thickness, the bobbins will roll from the ends to the back or front, in total disregard of the wishes and intentions of the operator, and will be an intermittent aggravation.

A pillow which is round like a globe, though good for keeping the bobbins in place, does not give a sufficiently flat surface unless its size be very cumbersome.

For large pieces of work, such as handkerchiefs, collars, etc., a pillow made by uniting two large circles of material with a narrow band of the same, when firmly stuffed, gives a very useful shape.

Pillows may be obtained at the principal drapers in the Midland and Western Lace Centres: or, if the expenditure of time is less an object than that of money, they may be made at home.

A first pillow is frequently required to be portable, so as to be easily carried between the lace class and the pupil's home, while it should be convenient for working: for these combined purposes, the following materials and measurements are recommended, as the results of experience.

Strong brown calico, free from dress or stiffness, is a useful material for the inner case. From this, take a strip 14 in. wide and 28 in. long, also two circles $3\frac{1}{2}$ in. in diameter. Seam the two short ends of the strip together, making a broad seam, easy to penetrate with a pin. Gather the two sides of the strip upon a $\frac{1}{4}$-in. turning; or hem them, making eyelet holes on either side of the seam, on the right side, and running cords or tapes through the hems. Turn the case wrong side out. Turn down a quarter of an inch round the two circles and draw up one gathered side to its size. Halve and quarter the gathered piece, and sew strongly to a circle. Proceed in the same manner with the second side, but only sew to half the circle.

Turn the case right side out, and stuff the pillow. The best material for this is straw cut into lengths of about 4 in., with all knots and hard pieces removed. Wheat straw, being stiff, is difficult to stuff evenly, but, that difficulty being surmounted, makes a good, firm, springy pillow.

The straw should be placed in the case by handfuls; each handful being so arranged as to lie in a flat layer on the last;

and should then be pressed and kneaded into the shape which it is wished the pillow should take.  As regards this shape—the ends should be well rounded.  The more gradual the curve from the working part of the pillow to the centre of the 3-in. circle, the better the bobbins will stay in their places when hanging over the ends.  What we may call the cylindrical part of the pillow, midway between the two circles, on which the pattern will be pinned, should be kept as even, smooth and hard as possible. No straw end must be allowed to poke up and raise a little hill ; and no $\frac{1}{2}$ in. of vacant space should allow a needful pin to seek in vain for point-hold.  When a quarter of the straw is in, the partly made pillow should be well beaten, with a mallet or rolling-pin, and then knelt upon or compressed in any convenient way.

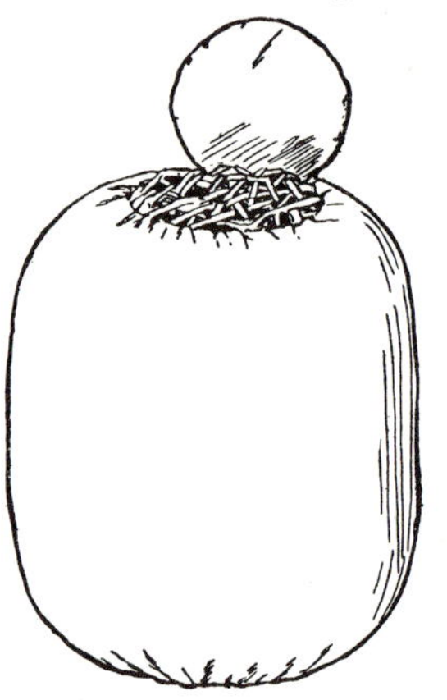

Fig. 1 - Making a Pillow

When half filled, this treatment should be repeated with redoubled energy ; and yet again and again as the filling approaches completion. (See Fig. 1.)  At the end of the filling, if the pillow is to prove a good one, the greatest difficulty should be experienced in forcing in the last handfuls.  A few hours spent on making the pillow perfect, will be well employed.  If made by hand, the harder the pillow is, the more comfortable a companion it will be.  With straw for stuffing, it is impossible to make it too hard without mechanical help.  Some pillows, however, bought from Bedford and Buckingham, being probably stuffed under hydraulic pressure, are somewhat too hard for the delicate Honiton-pins to penetrate.

A second cover is optional, but usual for those who take pride in the appearance of their pillow.  For this slip cover a washing material is very suitable, but whatever it may be, it must be easy for pins to go through.  The length of material cut for the outer cover should be about 30 in. ; and the width 16 in.  The two ends should be seamed together, making, as before, a broad seam, through which it is easy to send a pin.  A $\frac{3}{4}$-in. hem should be made at the two sides and cord, tape or ribbon run in the hems.  Two circles of the same material as the cover should be cut, hemmed and fastened with strong pins, one at each end of the pillow, over the smaller circles.  The loose cover is then slipped on and the ends drawn and tied.  In putting this on, it is well to see that the seams of the upper and under covers are nearly together, but do not coincide.

For a cushion of the flatter style : Cut two circles of strong, brown calico, of a size sufficiently large to take any pattern that may be required ; bearing in mind that collars may generally be made in halves, and handkerchiefs in quarters. A circle of thin wood, or very stiff cardboard, cut slightly smaller than the calico ones, will be found an assistance in keeping this cushion flat. A band of the calico 2½ in. wide, and sufficiently long to go round the other circles with at least an inch over, must also be provided. Make ½-in. turnings on the band lengthwise, and on one of the circles, and sew them together ; starting 2 in. from one end of the band and stopping at about the same dis-

Fig. 2 - Pillow stand

tance from the other. Cut the band to the right size and seam the two ends together. Then finish the sewing on of the band. This method enables the worker easily to adjust the size of the band to that of the circle. Turn the work with the rough edges inside and fit in the wooden circle. Make a ½-in. turning on the other calico circle and sew five-sixths of it to the free edge of the band. The stuffing should now be put in round and round the circumference, except, of course, against the opening through which it is introduced.

Like the stiffening at the bottom of the pillow, stuffing the circumference before any straw is left in the middle, is a help in keeping the pillow flat. Of course this flatness is only comparative. A well-filled cushion must have some slight roundness : but with care there need not be enough to prevent even a large pattern from setting in a satisfactory manner.

**Pillow Stands.**—These will be found most useful in keeping the round, or bolster-shaped, pillows steady for working.   As regards shape, the folding kinds are convenient ; but the larger lace depots will generally provide a variety of patterns both for the table and the floor.   (See Fig. 2.)

A lidless cardboard box of the right size and shape will answer except for strength and appearance ; while if covered in sateen or cretonne it may be found quite suitable, at least for a time. There is, however, no doubt that a stand which rests on the floor and can be raised and lowered as required is best for general use if not too cumbersome.

**Thread.**—In lace making, the most important material is the thread, which should be of pure linen.   This, in its finest numbers, is difficult to obtain, and costly, yet adds much more than its price to the value of the lace.   Cotton thread is beautifully white, and can easily be obtained in very fine sizes, and lace made with it looks very well till it is washed ; though an expert can at once tell the difference between it and that made with linen thread.   But, after it is washed, the cotton lace, being too soft, stretches and does not keep its shape well ; having a lax, plebeian appearance compared with well-made thread lace.

In some classes of lace in Belgium, a thick cotton thread is used for outlining flowers, etc., and is called a cordonnet.   This corresponds to the thick linen thread used in English lace for the same purpose, and largely known as the " gimp," or in Devon as the " shiney thread."

Very fine linen thread is most difficult to obtain, while evenly spun linen thread, well twisted and very fine, is rare indeed and very expensive.

The student of lace should certainly learn to distinguish between cotton and linen thread ; the best way of doing so being to compare the two with the microscope, as well as with the naked eye.

Cotton thread is more twisted and its fluff has a softer, more curly appearance **than** that of linen.   To the touch linen is colder, and in look more glossy than cotton.

A very good way of learning to distinguish the difference between them is to label several skeins of thread, some known to be cotton and others linen, of several degrees of fineness. Then mix them together and try to sort them correctly without seeing their labels.   When this can be done with certainty, the skeins may be cut, some threads drawn from each, and the exercise continued till single threads of fine numbers can be recognised with ease.

**Bobbins.**—For every kind of pillow lace, bobbins are necessary to hold the thread ; and very considerably do they differ.   Ribbon laces of the type of Lille, Valenciennes, and Maltese require heavy bobbins : and our workers in Bedford and Buckingham frequently use most interesting examples of elaborate workmanship, ornamented with metal and finished with beads strung on wire. Torchon and the coarser Guipure require large bobbins on which to accommodate their thick thread.

Brussels and Honiton, whose workers have the habit of passing the bobbin through a loop of their fine thread, are best made with a small plain bobbin of moderate weight. For this work the bobbin should have a smooth, round head, medium length of neck (perhaps an inch), plain body, not exceeding $\frac{1}{4}$-in. in diameter nor 3 in. in length, and ending in a point. (See Fig. 3.) As to material, soft wood is cheapest, but is too fibrous to polish quickly from wear, and so slip comfortably through the fingers. Bone is rather heavy, though some students prefer it. Boxwood

Fig. 3 - Bobbin

is perhaps the best choice, being smooth, light, and not too expensive.

**Pins.**—The pins used for the ribbon laces are rather long and moderately fine, with some having coloured glass heads by which to distinguish headings, footings, etc. Those for Honiton and Brussels should be fine and not too long.

No pins used for lace making should be liable to rust ; hence they should be obtained from a reliable dealer in lace supplies.

**Patterns.**—Patterns for pillow lace are pricked on tough paper, cardboard, or parchment. Japanese paper of good quality has been found strong and satisfactory. A flat wash of green applied before pricking the pattern will be likely to give comfort to weak eyes.

With a strong needle-pin two or three copies may be made at one pricking.

Old patterns may be obtained from the various lace centres or schools, or may be copied directly from old lace. It should be recognised that some lace patterns are copyright.

The beginner may do well to use only copied patterns till she learns the possibilities and limitations of her work. But as soon as she learns to understand what she can and, more especially, what she cannot do, it will be well for her to make a few simple patterns for herself. Beautiful designs may be traced from well-chosen leaves picked from the wayside and designs made for other purposes may be altered and adapted to the shape required.

In making collars, etc., the outline of the article in making should be traced on paper, and the sprays arranged to fill it in. Care should be taken that the design is well covered, and that there is little repetition of exact shapes, unless to produce certain effects.

The beginner should be careful not to put in too great a variety. Roses with their own leaves only, but with no single spray or leaf an exact copy of any other, in unskilled hands would be likely to make a prettier design than if mixed with other different flowers and leaves. The pattern should be evenly covered both for appearance and strength.

Many workers guard their patterns with jealous care: some designs are registered and can only be used with permission; while the frequent purchase of patterns becomes expensive, hence it is desirable to learn to make your own designs, which also give more individuality and freshness to your work.

Patterns for the Torchon and Guipure laces require to be traced with marks showing the path of the principal lines of work.

To copy an ordinary pattern, pin the paper for the copy smoothly upon the pillow with a long, stout pin at each corner driven into the head with the point inclining slightly towards the centre of the pattern. If more than one copy be made, see that the edges of all papers coincide. Pin down the pattern in the same way, leaving the margin as required.

Follow the lines of pinholes with the needle-pin, which must be held perpendicularly as each perforation is made, or the pinholes in the under patterns will not be in their exact places.

Look out for mistakes and see that they are not copied.

If a pattern must be altered, make an exact copy. Upon that draw the alterations, using ruler, set-square, and compasses if desirable. When you are satisfied, prick pinholes at the like distances to the rest of the pattern. From this copy your working pattern.

New patterns may be pricked with about ten pinholes to the inch for the finer laces.

Patterns for the Torchon and Guipure laces require to be traced with marks showing the path of the principal lines of work.

To copy a pattern from the lace, pin the latter firmly on a pillow, over paper ruled in very small squares, with the footing even with a line of the paper. Pin the outlines carefully in place, starting with the footing. Perforate every pinhole with a needle-pin, including those required for each mesh of net.

Remove the lace and make another copy on a fresh piece of squared paper, correcting all places where the pinholes are incorrect.

Then copy on paper, card, or parchment, by pinning down the squared paper over the other and pricking through each pinhole. If the style of lace should require it, draw the usual guide marks carefully.

**Needle-pins.**—An instrument much smaller than fingers is required to arrange the set of the threads of fine lace in process of

*Fig. 4 - Needlepin*

making: and to disentangle loops of thread from the heads of miscellaneous pins.

The implement in general use is called a needle-pin, and may be made with little difficulty. Choose a good match and cut off the head, splitting the end carefully for about half an inch. Introduce the eye of a number eight needle, pushing it up as far as it will go, and bind the end with thread in the same way as the handle of a cricket bat is treated. This is very springy and good for general use, but not firm enough for pricking patterns. For the latter purpose only two-thirds of the needle should be used and should be firmly set in a small handle by a tool-maker. (See Fig. 4.)

The match-made needle-pin was formerly used for making sewings, but has been largely superseded by calyx-eyed and other

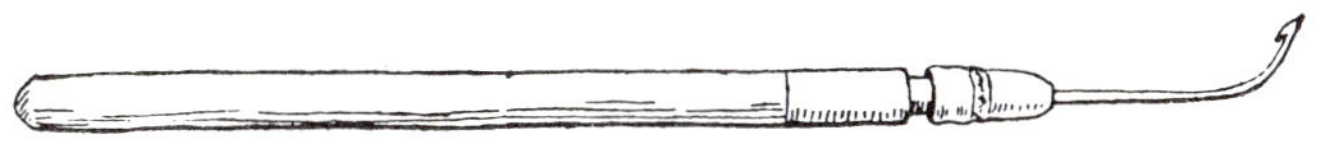

*Fig. 5 - Wigmakers Needle*

self-threading needles. Crochet hooks have been used for sewings, but are dangerous, being likely to catch on wrong threads and do mischief difficult to remedy. A wig-maker's needle, however, which is a curved and very delicate modification of the crochet hook, may be used as a tractor with greater success. (See Fig. 5.)

The Brussels workers use their needle-pins for sewing, and in some cases have them heated and slightly curved near the point.

**Leaf-stitch Pins.**—The writer introduces these on her own responsibility. She has found them useful for supporting the warp threads in leaf stitch ; especially when extra ones are used, and when a raised rib is made.   (See Fig. 6.)

Take a short hat-pin, with pliers, and heat, in a flame, near the glass head : fix the cool end in a vice firmly, and bend the

Fig. 6 – Leafstitch Pin

heated part round a pencil or thick knitting-pin, till, having formed a circle, the glass head is back in its old position in a line with the stem of the pin, pointing upwards when the pin is perpendicular.

In use the pin is stuck into the cushion as required, and the thread passed into the circle between the head and wire.

**Bobbin Winders.**—If lace be made for sale, or time a serious consideration, the purchase of a winder is advisable.   Two of these are in regular use : the old Turn, which under skilled management still answers our requirements fairly well ;  and a smaller machine, clamped to the table, and requiring a skeinholder to be used with it.

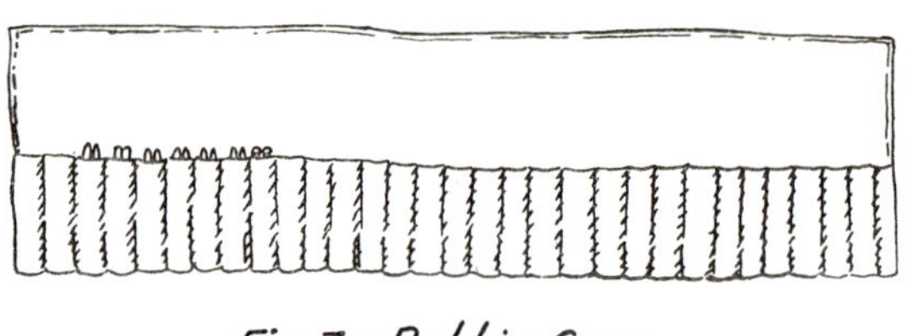

Fig. 7 – Bobbin Case

Also the brother of a lace student has made for the writer a machine having several advantages over the older forms.

**Bobbin Cases.**—These are almost necessary.  Without them the worker is apt to lose thread, time, and temper : for a threaded bobbin not under strict discipline is generally doing something its owner would rather it did not do.

Take a strip of washable material, say 1 yard long, and 12 in. wide.   Hem this, and turn up about 3 to 3½ in. along the strip, to form a pocket.   Sew up the sides and divide into compartments just large enough for two wound bobbins to slip in easily.   (See Fig. 7.)

Wound bobbins should be put in head first and others with

head exposed. The loose flap is folded over, and the case rolled up and tied with a tape, which should be firmly stitched near one end.

If much work be done, several cases of various sizes will be required.

**Carrying Cases.**—To be convenient, carrying cases should open widely, and be large enough for the pillow to slip in easily. Cut a strip of American cloth and one of sateen, or other material for lining, long enough to go round the pillow and overlap several inches, and rather wider than its length ; and bind together with braid. Cut two rounds of American cloth, and two of the lining, slightly larger in diameter than the pillow. Bind them with braid and sew them one to each side of the strip, starting at about 3 in. from one end, leaving half the circle free so that the pillow may slip in easily. Cut a strip of American cloth about 3 in. wide and long enough for a handle with 4 in. over. Fold the strip and bind the cut edge. Mark 2 in. from one end of the handle ; place the marked-off piece on the centre of one of the circles and stitch it round strongly, taking care that the position of the handle is convenient for carrying. Do the same with the other end and circle. Strings, or buttons and loops, should be provided for closing the flaps.

# CHAPTER III

# ELEMENTARY INSTRUCTION

**D**RESSING THE PILLOW.—To prepare (or technically to dress) the pillow, a strip of soft linen or a folded handkerchief should first be firmly pinned over its working part. The pillow should have been turned so that the seams in its cover are as far as possible from the pattern ; which is next pinned smoothly on the linen. A handkerchief, folded in half, should now be laid across the back of the pillow with the folded edge uppermost and covering the edge of the pattern. Each upper corner of

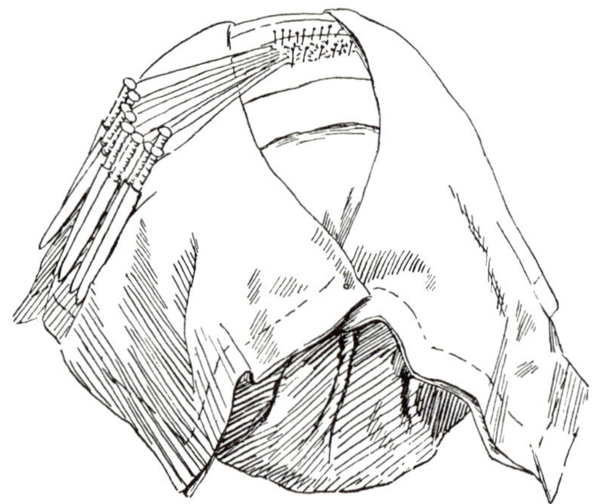

Fig. 8.—Dressing the Pillow

this is pinned on the centre of a circle of the pillow cover. This handkerchief is intended to keep clean any finished work: and should cover all pins and pattern edges close up to the part on which the worker is engaged ; being moved forwards as each fresh part of the pattern is completed. In the front of the pillow another handkerchief is pinned on, in the same way, leaving uncovered only that part of the pattern which is being made. (See Fig. 8.) When leaving the work for a moment, the upper flap of one of these handkerchiefs is spread over the work and bobbins, protecting them from dust and the intrusive fly. When definitely putting up, a large piece of muslin, or other washing material (an old blind will answer very well), should envelop the pillow and everything upon it. It should be securely fastened by pins or otherwise : so that deterioration from dust is rendered impossible.

**Bobbin Winding.**—Bobbins are usually wound and counted in pairs. To avoid knots, sufficient thread for the pair is cut off, and half of it wound on each bobbin. The length of thread used must depend on the class of lace in making. Where there is no cutting off and joining in of bobbins, they should be well filled

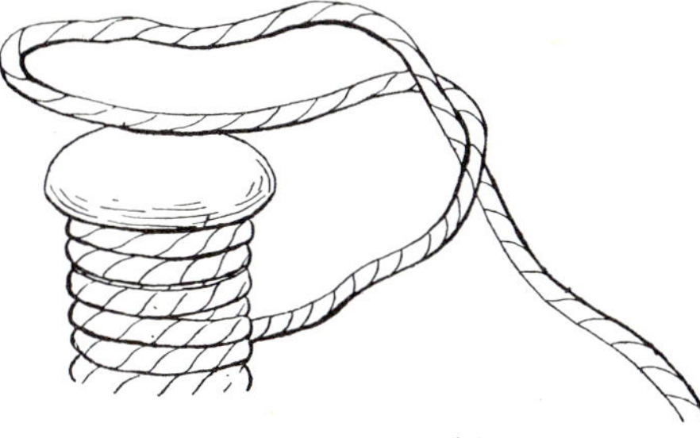

*Fig. 9 - Looping a Bobbin*

to avoid trouble and knots. On the contrary, where bobbins are frequently in hand for sewings, tying off and fastening on, the thread is apt to soil even with great care, and short windings are better.

In winding, take a bobbin in the left hand ; with the right hand lay an end of thread on the neck of the bobbin. Hold it there with the thumb of the left hand, and with the right hand wind the thread round the neck of the bobbin for five or six turns, passing the thread from your body and above the bobbin, beginning at the head of the bobbin, laying the thread evenly, and keeping a firm, regular tension. The winding may be finished by revolving the bobbin with the left hand, while the thread is held and guided by the right. When nearly half the thread has been wound, the bobbin must be firmly held by the left hand, while the right hand makes a loop near the head of the bobbin, by placing that part of the thread which is about 2 in. from the head across at right angles on the thread, about half an inch from the bobbin, with the part of the thread furthest from the bobbin pointing upwards, protruding at the bobbin's head. The loop is then placed over the head of the bobbin, an extra twist being given to it in doing so. (See Fig. 9.) The use of this loop is to prevent the bobbin from running down when suspended from the cushion. By the extra twist is meant putting the loop over, with the bobbin head through it, from the back. If it be twisted *too* much the thread will not run. The other half of the thread should now be wound in the same way, the companion bobbin looped and the pair hung on the cushion or stored in a clean box or case.

Instead of the usual loop the writer sometimes strings two very small beads upon the middle of the thread for each pair of bobbins, each bead having the thread passed twice through it. When a bobbin is wound the bead nearest is taken up and the thread crossing it loosened, run up close to the bobbin and passed over its head, the bead being then drawn up to the neck of the bobbin.

The method is effectual but takes time.

**Linen, Cloth or Whole Stitch.**—The first stitch to be mastered for every kind of pillow lace is linen or cloth stitch. For the ribbon laces it is used in footings, headings and ornamental spots and flowers, etc. : and for Brussels and Honiton it forms the greater part of the lace. It should be learned at once ; and so thoroughly that fingers as well as mind must always remember it. With threads of different colours, positions and movements are more easily followed.

Wind four bobbins with four different colours easily distinguished from each other and knot the four ends together. Fix a pin in a lace pillow, or large pin-cushion, so that half of it stands up from the surface. Hang the bobbins over this with two threads on either side and straighten the threads so that they do not cross.

Notice that one pair of bobbins is in the middle and another pair outside them. Begin with the middle pair; lift the left-hand bobbin over the right. Dividing the four bobbins into left and right pairs, lift each right-hand bobbin over its left-hand neighbour. End with the same movement that you began with ; with the middle pair lift the left-hand bobbin over the right. Thus :—

Left over right (middle pair).
Right over left (right-hand pair).
Right over left (left-hand pair).
Left over right (middle pair).
Lettering the bobbins *A, B, C* and *D* the positions will be :

$$ABCD.$$
$$ACBD.$$
$$ACDB.$$
$$CADB.$$
$$CDAB.$$

Original position *ABCD.*
Final position    *CDAB.*   (See Fig. 10.)

*A B* and *CD* keep their relative positions ; *A* on the left of *B* and *C* of *D*.

But the pair *A B* has worked through *CD* and is now in position to work through other pairs which may lie on its right.

Having completed the first stitch, take a pair of bobbins in each hand ; draw up the stitch close to the pin, and stick another pin between the two pairs of bobbins close to the last stitch. Repeat the above movements, placing a pin after each stitch, until they can be done mechanically : in fact, it is well to

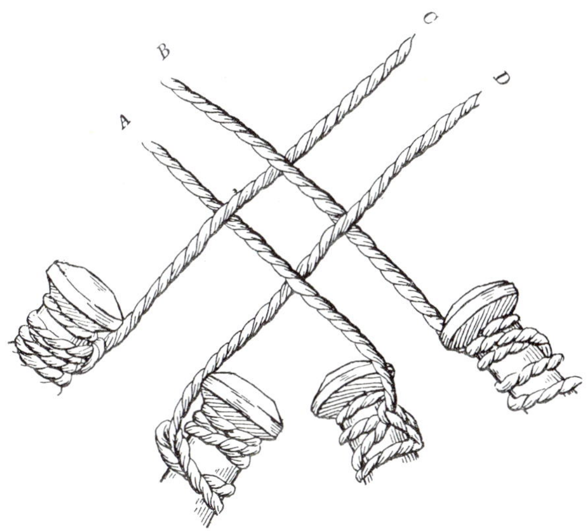

Fig. 10 – Linen, Cloth or Whole Stitch

make another 10 or 12 in. after the student feels proficient, before going on to the next stage.

**First Braid**.—This elementary work is used as a footing in many kinds of lace, and with modifications takes a large part in the manufacture of Brussels and Honiton, which, it should be borne in mind, is made wrong side outwards.

The pillow with its pins, bobbins and thread is a loom, on a very small scale. Some bobbins have their threads lying always parallel with the edges of the pattern, keeping the same position in relation to each other. These form the warps of the material. Other bobbins travel backwards and forwards through the warp and form the woof.

It is easier to learn the method of making the braid if the

thread on the warp bobbins is white and the three pairs of weavers, which take their turn in travelling, carry three colours forming a good contrast with each other. Thus any mistake is readily seen.

To make the pattern for the first braid, rule two parallel lines five-sixteenths of an inch apart on a piece of stout paper. Pierce each line with pinholes, about eight to the inch, and make one pinhole midway between the lines at their commencement. Put the letter *A* against this pinhole, *B* against the first hole on its left, and *C* against the first on the right.

Pin the pattern firmly, the edges being parallel with the ends of the pillow; running a strong pin through each corner of the pattern, inclining the point slightly towards the centre of the pattern and pushing it into the pillow up to its head. This gives a firm hold to the pins and prevents the pattern from shifting.

Wind three pairs of bobbins with white thread, and three pairs with colours. The threads are better not too fine.

Tie the bobbins together in pairs of like colour.

Place a pin in the middle hole *A*, running it from a third to half its length into the pillow. Hang the six bobbins with the white thread over the pin; placing each pair separately so that the threads do not cross each other. These are the warps. Hang a pair of coloured bobbins over the pin and place them to the right of the white ones. Hang another pair to the left of the white ones and the last pair to the left of these. These three pairs will be used as weavers.

Stick a pin in the *B* pinhole between the coloured threads and the white ones. Note that you have two pairs of bobbins outside the pin. Make a cloth stitch with these outer bobbins, twist each pair three times from right to left, and tighten the stitch against the pin by taking one pair in each hand and pulling in opposite directions. Lay the pair which is now at the left (which we will call red) back on the cushion, a little away from the others, and place the right-hand pair next to the white ones. Work a cloth stitch with this pair, which we will call green, and the next pair of white bobbins, then successively with the second and third pair. The green bobbins will now be on the *C* side of the white ones; twist them three times from right to left; put a pin in the *C* hole, taking care to have the threads of two pairs of bobbins and only two outside the pin: and make a cloth stitch with the coloured bobbins left on the *C* side (which we will take as blue). Twist each pair from right to left; tighten the stitch against the pin; lay the green bobbins back a little way from the others, and work the blue bobbins through to the *A* side.

Continue in the same manner, that is :—

Twist the weaver bobbins (which are coloured) three times as soon as they have worked through the white ones, and place a pin in the next pinhole, on the side at which they have arrived, with always four bobbin threads outside the pin. Next make a stitch with the pair of weavers found resting at that side and twist each pair three times. Lay the outer pair a little back and work through the centre bobbins with the pair next to them. (See Fig. 11.)

*Note.*—In lace making, all twists or crossings of thread are made from right to left.

After a few rows, the worker can see the reason for what has

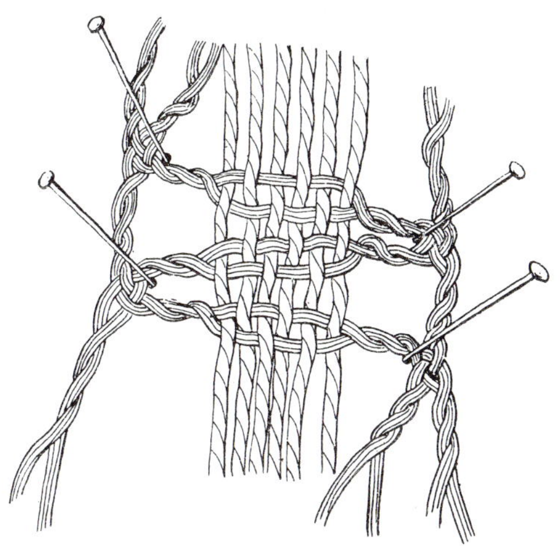

Fig. 11 - First Braid Warps light, Weavers shaded

been done. There is a muslin-like cloth in the middle of the braid which has been formed by passing the weavers from one side to the other, threading them in and out of the warps so as to make a wide plait. It will be seen that the open work at the edges is formed by cords to which tiny loops are fastened, and that this cord is made by the pair of bobbins left behind at every row. Also that half the loop fastened to it is made by the weavers from the other side, and the other half by those going towards the other side. It will be remembered that the weavers are exchanged at every row.

Much the same appearance may be made without this exchange, that is by keeping, say, the green bobbins always on one side, the blue at the other, while the red work ever backwards and forwards. However, this method would produce certain drawbacks, both to appearance and durability. For, after the pin has been stuck and the stitch and twists made, if the same weavers that came across are to return, instead of laying them back as usual they must be brought forward, and if they be the reds, crossed over the green or blue, which lie ready to make the return journey. Or, in place of the crossing, the reds may make a second stitch with the greens or blues ; which will bring them into the right position for the return. But both the crossing and the second stitch are unsatisfactory. Either would give a slight clumsiness of appearance to the edge and in either case the cord being always made by the same bobbins would be continuous with the loops as it were threaded upon it and liable to slide from their exact position.

When an ornamental loop is formed at the edge the second stitch at the edge is made, but the loop gives lightness to the appearance, and the ordinary edge on the opposite side of the braid, etc., gives stability.

**Ordinary Braid.**—When possible, two bobbins should be wound on one thread (p. 17) without knots, but if wound separately the threads must be knotted together and the knots arranged as required. If the piece of work be small, it may be worth while to wind the knot on one of the bobbins with enough thread on the working side of it to finish the spray, etc. Otherwise the knot should be so placed that it may not get in the way too soon, but be taken out at the worker's convenience. The knots can be thus disposed of one or two at a time with a few rows in between.

The pattern must be firmly pinned upon the pillow (p. 16), running evenly round it. In the case of a braid or edging lace, a second pattern may be pinned at the end of the first ; and by repeating this any length required can be made without removing the work from the pillow.

Having tied the bobbins and wound up the knots to their correct places, a pin must be stuck at the upper end of the pattern, midway between the two rows.

Take a pair of bobbins and hang it over the pin, placing the bobbin without a knot on the left side as a weaver. Hang three other pairs in the same way ; each pair being hung evenly outside the last. The four bobbins without knots, for weavers, will lie on the left, and those with knots, for warps, on the right. Hang the next pair with the knotless bobbin for a weaver on the right and the other on the opposite side of the pin, between the weavers and warps. Hang the next pair in the same way. There will now be six warps in the centre, four weavers on the left and two on the right. Any further bobbins should be hung in the centre, with an equal number of bobbins on either side of them, with the exception of a pair, wound with a thick thread and called gimps, which must be placed on either side between the weavers and the warp, their mission being to outline the linen work and give it distinction.  Twist each pair of weavers three times.

The number of bobbins required for a braid varies with its width and the fineness of the thread.  For braid a quarter of an inch wide made with an ordinary fine thread, about twelve will be needed, adding about six for every eighth of an inch extra width.  About an eighth of an inch should be taken by the two edges, in working which six bobbins are used.

The first stitch is made on the side on which are the four weavers, in this case on the left.  If there be more holes on one side than the other, begin on the side on which are the most holes, if there be no special reason to the contrary.  Before commencing, see that your weavers are properly twisted.  Put a pin in the first hole, make a stitch, twist both pairs three times and lay back the outside pair.  Work the inside pair through the warp bobbins, twist, and make a stitch with the resting weavers on that side, after putting in a pin.  Always pull up the threads against the pin after dealing with the resting weavers to prevent slackness.

Proceed as above till a knot is to be removed, or the work widens or narrows sufficiently to make it necessary to add, or throw out, bobbins.

**Curved Braid.**—When working a curved pattern where the row of pinholes for the outside edge is much longer than that for the inside, it is first necessary to see if it be possible to rearrange the pinholes and, by putting the outside ones further apart, or those inside nearer together (or both), to work the curve in the ordinary way.

The points to be considered are these :—

The outside edge must not have the pinholes so far apart that the warps catch the eye as bare threads.

The inside holes must not be so crowded as to lose the distinctive character of the edge.  The cord and each separate loop should be distinguishable, though closer together than on the outer edge.

The weavers should cross so that their threads lie in a line drawn from the outer loop formed by them to the centre of the curve.

Even if there be found too great a disproportion between the number of holes in the outer and inner curves to meet the difficulty entirely by rearrangement ;  yet such planning will generally be of considerable assistance.

After having arranged the pinholes in the best possible way, they should be counted and the proportion noted ; the counting beginning from the spot where the curve commences or changes.

We will suppose the number of holes in the outer edge to be sixteen, and those of the inner edge to be eight.

The character of the curve must now be noted ; if it be a long curve, and the same throughout its length, each pinhole must be used twice ; which gives the required proportion of eight to sixteen or one to two.

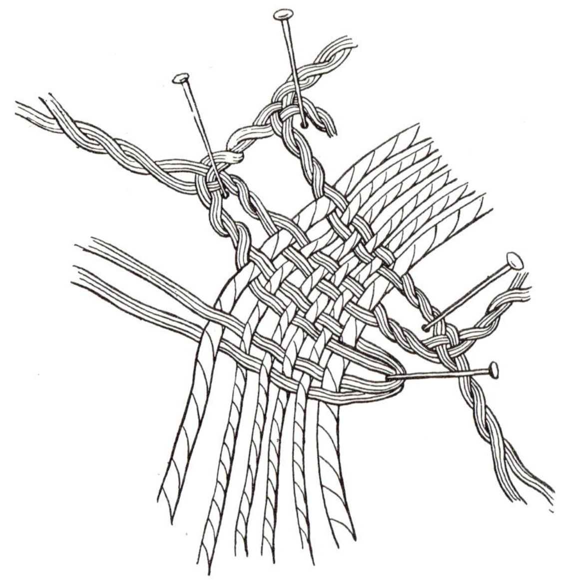

Fig. 12 – Curved Braid – First Stage

If the curve be abrupt, the holes in the sharper part of the inner curve must be used more frequently, and those in the shallower parts less. For this, the centre hole in the inner part of the sharpest curve can be used three times ; the four holes, two on either side of that, may be taken twice each, which gives us six out of the eight extra holes required. One hole on either side of the seven we have arranged, may be now taken as usual, that is used once, and the two next to those taken twice, which will give the eight extra holes.

Having decided how many times we will use each hole, and (if at first necessary) noted the number against each hole in pencil, the lace is worked as usual until the first hole is reached which is to be used twice, when the weavers that have just worked through must be crossed once only, for much twisting would thicken the edge of the clothwork and make it look clumsy. A pin is now inserted as usual, with four bobbin threads outside it, and the bobbins which have just worked across are taken back again (without touching the resting weavers) to the outer side, which is worked as usual.  (See Fig. 12.)  When the inner side is reached again the last pin is removed, and replaced with

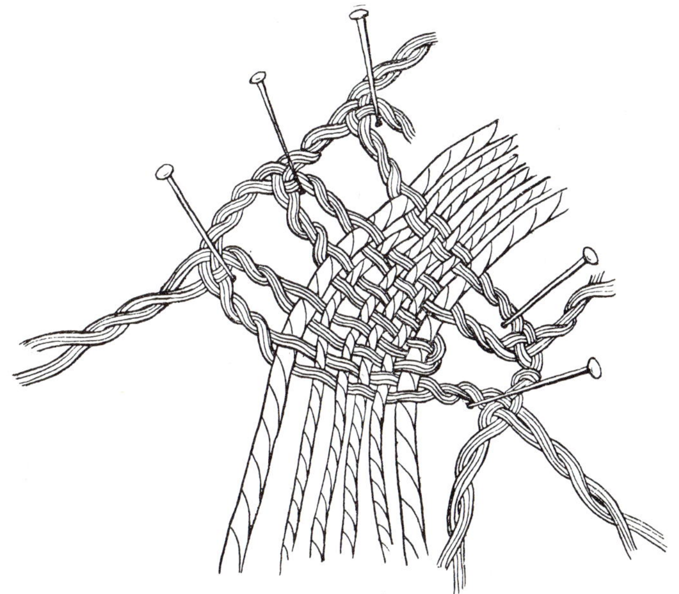

Fig. 13 — Curved Braid _ Second Stage

the usual four bobbin threads outside it.  (See Fig. 13.)  Looking closely, there may be seen, behind the pin, the loop which was formed round it and released on its removal.  This looks untidy, but is made to disappear by pulling the weavers resting on the opposite side, while a pair or so of warp bobbins nearest to the loop are held with a slight tension to prevent the edge of the clothwork from being drawn out of shape.

If only one extra hole is required at this spot, the edge is finished in the usual way, but if more are needed the weavers nearest the pin must be crossed once and worked again to the outer side without touching those resting at the inner edge.

In fact, so many as are the extra holes needed for any pin, so many times must the weavers come across and make a loose loop, to be afterwards pulled up.

This method has been used for generations and is easy to work when the ordinary edge is made. Should, however, the edge be ornamented with " picots " the loop cannot be pulled up, because the same bobbins which made it wound their thread round a pin on the other side and no tension on the weavers could have any effect on it.

In this case, when a hole should be used more than once a " false pinhole " is made at about the width of a small pin's head inside it and the pin is at first placed in this instead of the proper hole. When the extra number of holes have been used and the weavers come to the pinhole for the last time, the pin is placed in the edge hole as usual. Each time the pin is lifted from the " false pinhole " the two nearest warps are pulled outwards until they touch the top of the loop.

Expert workers have another method. On arriving at an edge where they do not wish to use a pinhole, they employ the stout edging thread called gimp and cross their weavers round it. The weaver which lies under the gimp (after both weavers have worked through it) is brought over it, and the one which lies over it is passed underneath it. They are then pulled up while the gimp is held firmly. The thread which passes under must lie next to the gimp and the one that goes over second. The bobbin which pairs with the gimp is passed over the weaver next to it and under the other, and the work is ready to proceed as usual : care being taken at the opposite edge for two rows lest the weavers should draw the gimp round which they were passed out of place.

When the pattern has a very acute angle, and when many bobbins are employed, yet another method may be used. Take, for example, the point of a leaf which has a row of pinholes as midrib and which is to be worked up one side and down the other. The work on the outside edge of the leaf is done in the usual way, but the inside row of pinholes have no connecting cord, there being no resting weavers left on that side, the weavers from the opposite side always returning to it after passing their cord round a pin.

When the last midrib pinhole is reached, it is worked as usual and the weavers taken to the outside, when the edge is made and the return weavers brought across. The weavers are then laid down with their threads next to the pin : and the pair of warps next to them through which they have just moved are taken for weavers. These are worked to the outside edge, which is made and the return row continued till the pair of weavers next the pin is reached. These are not used, but the weavers in hand are laid beside them. The pair of warps lying next through which the weavers have just passed are now taken, worked to the outer edge, the return row made and the weavers in hand laid down beside those used before, while again the two warps last in hand are taken as weavers.

This method is continued until the centre pinhole (or one of the pair of centre pinholes) at the sharpest part of the curve has been worked, the return row made and the weavers in use laid down by the ones that worked the last return row.

Then the process is begun again. The pair of weavers first laid down by the side of the pin are taken worked to the edge, the return row made and the weavers laid down again by the side of the pin. The other pairs are taken in succession as they were before; this being continued until that pinhole is reached

Fig. 14 - Pattern of Sprig

which lies at the outer edge, next before the one level with the upper inside pinhole. The turning is then complete and in the return row the weavers are not laid down, but sewn into the uppermost central loop. The pin, removed for the sewing, is replaced and the weavers taken to the outside edge. A sewing is made into each central loop.

Two good points of this turning are :—

The inside curve is well filled and flat. When the bobbins are skilfully pulled and adjusted there is little open space above the highest centre pin.

Also, the warp bobbins next to the outside edge are not disturbed, and it is they that are most conspicuous; the changes among the inner ones do not attract much attention.

**Making a Sprig.**—The reduced pattern here given is very simple, and of a style much used in Brussels, where it was purchased many years ago. (See Fig. 14.)

Two methods are suggested for working it, the Brussels and the Honiton.

For the Brussels' mode, commence with the centre of the largest rose, at the beginning of the longest and narrowest of the three divisions. Hang on (p. 22) six pairs of fine-thread bobbins, and either a pair of gimps, or one gimp for the outer edge paired with a fine-thread companion. Work the centre and sew repeatedly to its commencement, draw the threads together and pass round them one weaver to the right and another to the left. Tie them twice. Lay the threads out neatly on the nearest curve of the outer circle. Work round the outer circle in linen stitch, half stitch, or other ornamental clothwork (p. 59), making picots (p. 44) where desired. Tie and cut off (p. 32). Hang five pairs of fine-thread bobbins on the centre circle of the smallest rose (p. 22). Work round in stem stitch and sew firmly. Lay out the threads on the commencement of the outer circle. Add two pairs of fine and one pair of gimps, or one gimp for the outside with a fine companion (p. 31). Spread out with care and work the outer circle in stemstitch, weaving the outer gimp over and under the fine threads to the centre and back to the edge to mark each petal ; and sewing strongly to the centre circle each time the weavers cross to it. Sew the end of the circle to the beginning. Throw out the gimp and all bobbins but five pairs (p. 31) and work stem stitch to the main stem of the sprig, and up again to the branch of three leaves. Work the two lower leaves in raised work (p. 53), throwing off and adding bobbins as required ; work up in stem stitch to the top leaf ; make that also in raised work. Tie and cut off.

Hang seven pairs at the stem end of the wide leaf with gimp as before, and work up one side of the leaf and down the other (p. 26). Tie and cut off.

Hang five pairs on the end of the smaller tendril, and work in stem stitch to where it touches the middle-sized rose, and up the larger tendril, making the two circles, fastening off neatly at the end and cutting off.

Hang five pairs to the centre of the middle rose ; work the inner round in stem stitch (p. 79, 4A). Sew to the beginning. Work round the outer curves, making the inner turns as flat as possible and sewing each turn strongly to the centre. Sew the last turn strongly to the first and work the flower stem to where it touches the main one. Tie and cut off.

Hang five pairs on the large rose, where the stem starts ; and work down in stem stitch, sewing to the flower stalk and along the large leaf. Crossing the stem of the branch of small leaves and the small flower, sew repeatedly to it. Continue the stem, making the small circle, and fastening off neatly.

Put in a square leaf-filling (p. 101) to the centre of the smallest rose. Work Lille net (p. 83) or small leaf fillings inside the outer curves of the large rose ; and a six-strand cobweb with twisted bars in its centre.

The Honiton way is different. The tendril and curls may be left out. The large rose can be worked as before.

Five pairs of bobbins are hung to the end of the stem, and stem stitch worked to the small leaves, which are made in raised work (p. 53), the top leaf first. A second stem is run over the first and sewn to it every second or third row, till the main stem is reached. The stem is worked to the small rose, which is made as before and the extra bobbins thrown back. A second stem is now worked over the first to the main stem, and up to the large leaf, which is worked up the stem side and down the outer side (p. 26), the stem being afterwards run up and sewn to the leaf.

The stem and middle rose may be worked as before, but then a second stem is made over the first to the main stem. This is continued to the rose, strongly sewn to it and cut off. The fillings may be as before.

There are many ways of working even so simple a pattern as this : but the foregoing will give an idea of some elementary methods in vogue in Belgium and Devon.

**Taking Out Knots.**—Knots in certain kinds of lace making must be made fairly often and if left on the finished work would be both conspicuous and untidy, hence it is the custom to remove them, which is a simple process.

A pin should be inserted in the cushion above the part in working (or one of the pins already set and used may be employed). Then the bobbin with the knot is lifted, its thread put round the pin, and replaced in its original position. Care must, of course, be taken that the pin is far enough off to ensure that the knot is well above the place where the thread comes again into the work.

The long loop which is thus formed must not be cut until after the formation of a fairly sharp curve, some fancy stitch which will take off the strain on the thread, or a sufficiently long piece of work to do the same. If this be forgotten, when tension is put on the bobbin whose knot was removed, its thread might pull bodily out, leaving a ladder in its place. In which case the thread may be darned in again with a fine needle.

Knots should not be removed from the edge of a lace ; the cut thread detracting both from its appearance and strength. In the case of a knot in a weaver, work it from the edge past the gimp and perhaps the next pair and then take out its knot or change it with a warp without a knot.

To change : when the knotted weaver has passed in the ordinary course of work, under the bobbin selected to take its place, it should be held back over it with one hand while the warp bobbin is picked up with the other.   The knotted bobbin is then dropped into the warp's place and the work proceeds as usual.   If the weaver has passed over instead of under the warp, it must be held down in front of it while the warp is lifted to use as a weaver and then the weaver dropped into place as above.

**Sewings.**—" Sewing " in pillow lace has a meaning quite

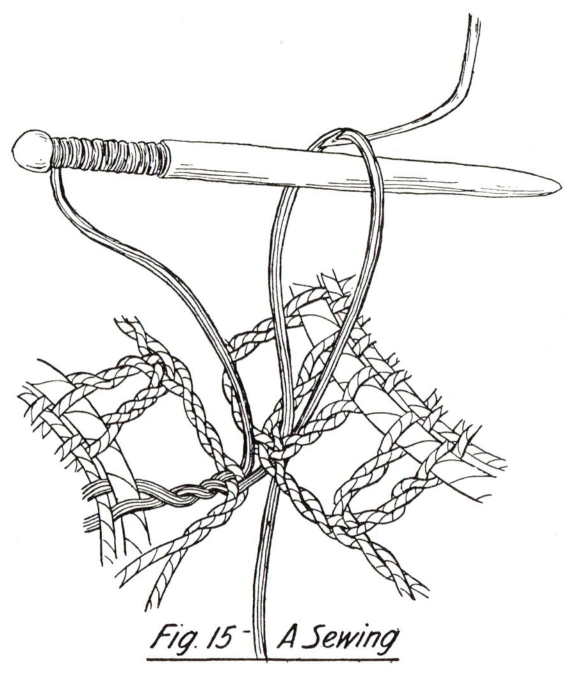

Fig. 15 — A Sewing

different from its employment in needle point and common use ; it denotes a distinct method.

The use of this method practically makes the two parts of lace thus connected into one.   Hence, if there is any probability that they may afterwards have to be detached for repair or alteration, it will be better to unite them in a less permanent way, say with a needle, or by means of a bar, net, or filling : or by sewings made with a detached pair of bobbins.

To take a sewing, the weavers must be worked to the pinhole nearest the spot where the junction is to be made ;  and the stitch made as usual with the resting weavers. The weavers in hand are twisted once or twice and the thread of one of them drawn through the nearest loop in the edge of the part to which junction is to be made, with a needle-pin, self-threading needle or other tractor forming a long loop. (See Fig. 15.) Through this is passed the companion bobbin ; both bobbins are pulled up and adjusted, twisted once or twice and laid down. A pin is set, both in the usual hole and the one belonging to the loop into which the sewing was taken, and the return made with the bobbins not used for sewing with those in fact which are habitually employed.

As regards instruments :—

The needle-pin has been used for generations, both at home and abroad and, in skilled hands, is sufficient.

A calyx-eyed needle is quick and certain, easy to thread by pressing the thread on the top of the needle ; and to unthread by bending back the thread passed through the eye and pressing it down on the top as in threading. Some workers use crochet hooks, but they are apt to catch in unwished threads and damage the work. A wig-maker's needle, however, which is a curved and delicately constructed hook, if carefully used, makes a quite satisfactory tractor.

Whatever instrument is generally used, it is well to have a self-threading needle at hand, in case of a difficult sewing.


## THROWING OFF AND ADDING BOBBINS

### IN DUCHESSE, BRUGES AND HONITON

To throw off a bobbin, lay it back so that it hangs on the part of the pillow opposite to the bobbins in use. The threads are not cut until the portion in hand is completed. Care must be taken in choosing which bobbins to throw out. In looking at the finished work, the eye follows the line of the threads, and stopped threads give the effect of shading.

The above remark applies equally to the addition of fresh bobbins. Brought in at wrong places, they throw leaf or flower out of shape.

Of adding fresh bobbins there are various methods, of which the one first to be given is that in general use.

Hang a pair of bobbins over a pin and drop them into the place required. Work a few rows, remove the pin and pull up the loop.

Hang the bobbins on the thread of a weaver where needed

or least observed (on that which will be the lower when worked across), giving them support until three or four rows have been worked to prevent dragging the weaver's thread.

Extra weavers may be hung on a gimp, but are best worked through the warps before making an edge, or the gimp may be pulled out of place.

In working a curve where extra bobbins are wanted, two pairs may be hung over a pin outside the edge and a stitch made between the nearest pair of these and the resting weavers ; which will then lie beneath the two new pairs. Twist the new pair nearest the work three times and work them across as weavers, dropping them separately near the inner gimp. Remove the pin supporting the new bobbins, place it in the next outer pin-hole of the pattern and twist both pairs of bobbins on that side. Lay back the new pair as resting weavers and work across with the other pair, dropping them separately as before. Unless the threads are crowded at the inner curve this manœuvre might show.

**Fastening Off.**—There are two ways of fastening off in constant use.

With the first, each pair of bobbins is tied separately first. Then open out one pair and lay the others between them. Cross the opened-out bobbins and pass them beneath the bundle of threads several times, drawing up and arranging the thread with care. Tie the pair used for binding twice, making a reliable knot and cut off the whole bunch. A good worker will vary a little by sewing to a neighbouring edge, or by extra ties, but that is the principle—Tie the bobbins round strongly and cut them off.

For a wide piece of work the other way is better, but many use it habitually. In this method the two bobbins composing each pair are tied together. Then an outside pair is taken, tied once with the nearest pair and in succession with the second, third and every other pair. A second tie with the same two pairs is only made with the last ones, and when this has been carefully made and tightened the bobbins may be cut off.

There is a scientific way of cutting off bobbins which leaves them tied in pairs. This can be done quickly, and, to a novice, has almost the appearance of a conjuring trick. There are four movements to the complete action, which must be carried out with very loose scissors.

1. Place the points of the scissors under the threads of two bobbins from the right.

2. Lift the scissors with the threads across, turning their points over the bobbins and then under the threads from which they hang. This forms a loop between the bobbins and the lace.

3. Support the bobbins with the left hand, and with the points

of the scissors seize the threads above them and draw them through the loop.

4. Cut the threads of the loop, draw away the tied threads and tighten them.

The difficulty here lies in the third movement. The loop sometimes lies rather high up and needs a judicious shake nearer to the points : or is too near the points and must be eased to open them : or the scissors are not loose enough and so cut the threads prematurely, instead of picking them up.

If, in the second movement, the points of the scissors be pointed to the lace instead of to the bobbins, when the threads are cut and the bobbins drawn away, it will be found that the knot is on the threads hanging from the lace and that the bobbins are unconnected !

## INVISIBLE HANGING ON

**Plain.**—The writer believes both this and the following section to describe new methods, or rather methods invented by herself and only known through her own pupils. She has not found any traces of such ways of commencing or finishing in English or foreign museums, or in any lace, ancient or modern, which she has had the opportunity of examining.

These methods may be found very widely useful to good workers; allowing many patterns to be easily worked, which, without them, would be practically unmanageable.

An invisible commencement is desirable for the tip of a petal, a leaf or the point of a conventional ornament. The system of working is as follows :—

Set a pin in the centre pinhole. Take two pairs of bobbins and hold one of each pair in the right and the other in the left hand. Twist the threads three times and hang them over the pin, so that their threads lie over the pattern on the front of the pillow. (See Fig. 16.)

Take another two pairs in the same way, twist them three times, and lay them down across the back of the pin.

Make a stitch between the left-hand pairs of these and of the two pairs hung over the pin. Pull up the stitch to the pin. Twist each pair three times and lay them down, the outside pair rather far back, the inside pair with the threads passing down the middle of the pattern.

These threads hanging down in front are the warp bobbins and those running across the back of the pin the resting weavers which make the cord.

The twist made by each two pairs before stitching with the resting weavers forms afterwards half the loop hanging on the cord ; and the twist given after the stitch before laying the warps in their place finishes the other half.

Set a pin on the left of the centre, inside the threads of the

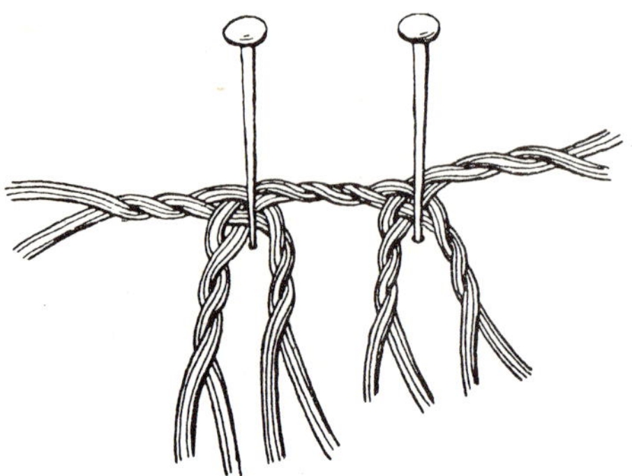

*Fig. 16 – Invisible Hanging On – First Stage*

resting weavers. Twist two more pairs the same as before and hang them over the last pin. Stitch the outside pair with the resting weavers and make the usual twists. Put back the outside pair and lay the other with the warp bobbins.

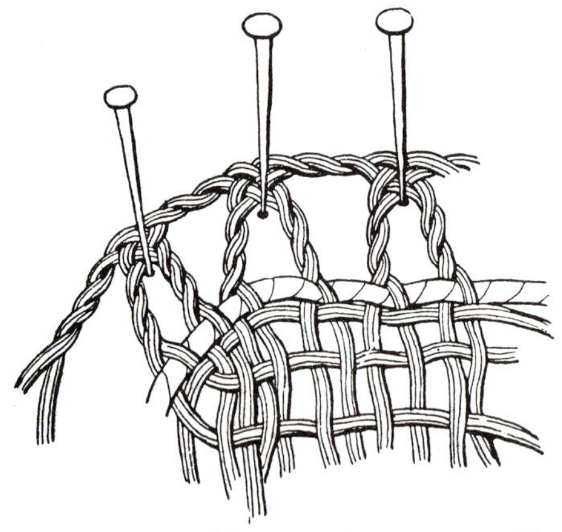

*Fig. 17 – Invisible Hanging On – 2nd Stage*

Set a pin in the next hole on the right of the centre and follow the same method as with the pin on the left.

Now examine the work : if it be a shallow curve and a wide

piece of work, it may be better to hang more bobbins in the next hole on one or both sides.

But if ten pairs will be, at present, enough for the work, take one pair of gimp bobbins and one pair of fine thread and place them together as before, but without twisting. Support them, temporarily on a pin set near the work on the right-hand side. Work them through the warp bobbins from right to left with the gimp on the left of the fine thread.

Support the gimp and its companion bobbin on a pin at the left of the work. Take the last pair of warps through which they passed, as weavers, and work them through to the right ; first laying the gimp and its companion bobbin (temporarily supported on the right-hand pin) by the side of the other warps. Make the edge and return ; first laying the right-hand gimp and its companion in their places with the other warps. (See Fig. 17.)

Instead of the above method of supplying weavers, if an extra pair of bobbins will not be too many, one may be hung on the left-hand gimp (before removing the supporting pin), twisted, three times, stitched with the edge, pair, and carefully adjusted, when the work may proceed as usual, the gimp and its companion being laid with the other warps before the weavers work through to the right. The gimp pairs on both sides will need support, or great care, until the weavers have worked through both pairs and have made the edge on either side. Great care must be taken that the gimp is not drawn from its position.

If the first method be preferred and no gimp be used, two pairs of fine bobbins may be worked through in the same way that the gimp pair were used, but from left to right. The edge may be made with them, and the work continued as usual, but care must be taken on the first return of the weavers to adjust the fresh pair on the left, after removing the supporting pin, before and after working through them.

**With Picots.**—When an open edge is to be made between the picots and the clothwork, a pin may be set in the centre hole, and two pairs twisted together six times and arranged as for hanging on with the ordinary edge (p. 33). Hang them over the pin and then of the left-hand pair pass the right bobbin under the right-hand pair and the left bobbin over it, laying it on the left of its companion. In this way the pair that was on the right is now on the left, having passed between the bobbins of the left pair. (See Fig. 18.) This makes the picot. Pull up both pairs. Take two fresh pairs, twisted as usual. Support their thread temporarily on a pin, and with the pair nearest the picot work through both pairs of picot bobbins and twist three times. This makes the cord of the open edge. Twist the two pairs which hang from the pin each three times, forming the loop between the cord and the clothwork.  Set another pin carrying two pairs of twisted bobbins next the centre one with the cord bobbins between it and the first pin and pass the right pair through the left as before.  Take the pair of cord bobbins next the new picot and work with them through the picot bobbins, outwards, twist them and each pair of picot bobbins.

When enough bobbins have been put on, the methods of adding gimp and commencing are the same as for ordinary edge.  For picots with no open edge hang upon each pin the two pairs twisted, and the right pair passed through the left, as above, until enough bobbins have been added.

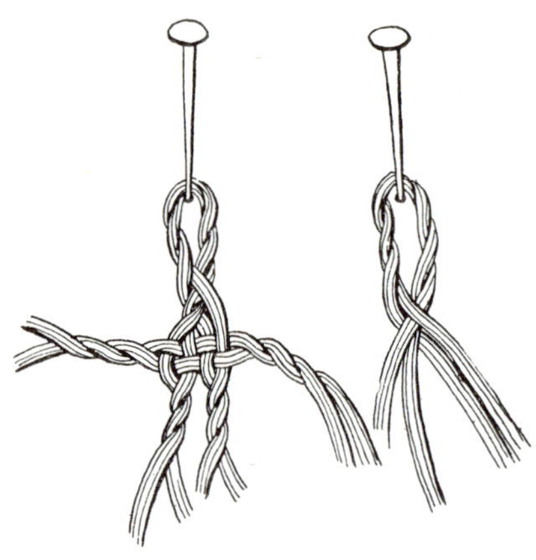

Fig. 18 — *Invisible Hanging On with Picots*

Put two pairs together, as usual, but without twisting, support them on a pin on the left-hand side and with the right-hand pair work through the picot bobbins from left to right.  Pass the gimp through with a companion bobbin, leaving a pair untouched on either side and start according to the directions for invisible hanging on with ordinary edge (p. 33).  When there is no open edge a pair of warps must lie outside the gimps with which to finish the picots.

**Unseen Finishing.**—To finish off a sprig, etc., of lace so that it has a continuous open work, or other, edge ;  and so that on the right side there is no indication of the whereabouts of the cut ends of the threads of which it is composed, is one of the most difficult problems which present themselves to an expert lace-maker.

The method described here was worked out by the writer, who believes that with care and a little practice it will be found to meet requirements.

Should the work narrow near the end, unnecessary bobbins should be thrown back.  Specially should one pair be laid back in the last row but one, near the edge from which the weavers are working.

Before working the last row, count the number of pinholes and of bobbins.  The pairs of bobbins should number one more than the holes.  If there be too many bobbins it is sometimes possible to rearrange the pinholes and get in one or two more.  Or, if not, the extra bobbins must be thrown back.  On the other hand, if the pinholes be too numerous they may be rearranged to lessen the number.

The relative number of bobbin pairs and holes being correct, work the last row and make the edge.

Instead of returning as usual, twist the weavers, lay them back and stitch them with the pair laid back specially in the last row but one, after passing the gimp under one weaver and over the other.  Lay back the weavers when stitched and place the Special Pair where they may be easily distinguished and used, for they have to stitch with every pair before it is thrown back.

Take the pair of warps next to the pin last set as weavers, pass them through the gimp, twist them and make the edge.  After twisting, pass the returning weavers through the gimp, stitch with the Special Pair and lay back.

Repeat with each pair of warps.

Having done this there should be left beside the gimps one pinhole and two pairs of bobbins, the resting bobbins from each edge.

Set a pin in the hole, see that each pair has been twisted, and make a stitch at the back of the pin.  Twist each pair and pass each separately through a gimp, stitch each with the Special Pair and lay it back.

If any bobbins were thrown back just before the last ordinary row, they should be picked up while the finishing edge is being made, as the work is brought level with them, worked through the Special Pair and laid back.

The pillow should now be turned, the Special Pair again worked through all the pairs put back from the finishing row, and then pulled up enough to draw the threads away from the edge, and to keep them from being seen on the right side.  One of the middle pairs may be passed round both the gimps, tied and cut off.  Or a pair from each end may be passed round a single gimp tied and cut off.  The rest of the pairs may then be tied and cut off.  Or the Special Pair may be tied, twice bound round the other threads, one going to the right and the other to the left, tied again and cut off.

The aim in the final tying off is compactness, flatness and security of fastening.

CHAPTER IV

# HOW TO BEGIN

**H**ONITON AND BRUSSELS.—In this class of lace the flowers and other ornamental parts, which comprise the pattern, are formed first ; and in case of detachable portions, known as sprigs, are stored until a sufficient number have been formed to complete the desired amount of work. Continuous borders, however, even where sprigs are used to complete the design, are generally filled in with the grounding and completed as soon as a convenient section is ready.

When the sprigs have been stored, before they are grounded they must be firmly pinned down upon their original pattern or they may be drawn out of shape. Even then the greatest care must be taken that the tension of the ground, whether of bars or net, shall be exact, neither loose to rise away from the flat surface, nor tight to spoil some graceful curve. If a net ground be used the meshes should be exactly perpendicular, horizontal or diagonal with the footing and should be all of the same size.

Before attempting to commence working the student should consider the pattern thoroughly, to decide which parts should be in plain linen stitch and which ornamental ; bearing in mind that there is little more attractive than plain clothwork, well made of fine linen thread which, in its dainty simplicity, should largely predominate.

Although the student may be able to make a great variety of intricate and beautiful stitches, the lace should not be regarded mainly as a means of displaying them. Were the whole, or even too great a proportion of the lace taken up by fancy stitches, however beautiful, difficult, or new (which last perhaps offer the greatest temptation), the work would lose its character and have a much commoner appearance.

The worker should strive to give both unity and variety to her production.

The first may be achieved by a broad treatment ; certain prominent parts of the design, repeated throughout, having always the same or similar working, while variety may be given by marking and accentuating slight differences of flower or ornament by different stitches.

The general grounding should be alike throughout, but if a

part of the ground be cut off by the design the treatment may differ. For instance, some very beautiful lace has been worked with a fine-meshed Lille net extending from the footing to the sprays, while amongst the latter the grounding has been of irregular bars with picots : giving an effect both unique and artistic. Two sizes of mesh are sometimes used for grounding net, in which case the finer mesh should have the smaller space allotted to it. In no case should the extent of the finer and more open mesh be equal—the effect would not be good.

Sometimes small spaces are cut off from the rest and may be treated individually, each having some difference in its filling, though a connecting link should be kept with all : the object ever being not so much to astonish by intricacy and variety, as to charm by true artistic balance. In this, as in all other really beautiful work, the artist must exercise some amount of self-repression.

Having decided the general treatment as to stitches and grounding, notes being made of everything which it may be possible to forget, the knotty point must be decided as to whether the pattern in certain places shall be worked in pieces (*i.e.* sprigs) or run on. It is quicker and stronger to run on without break : but, on the other hand, it is sometimes convenient to find the sprays detachable. In years to come, the lace may pass into the hands of the repairer or transferrer and it is well to make the work of those useful persons as easy as other considerations will permit.

An ample supply of suitable pins should be stuck on a small, soft cushion and pinned on a convenient spot on the pillow. Enough bobbins for the work (and a few over) should be wound, and those not immediately required stored in a clean bobbin case.

The clothwork may then be carefully made and the fillings put in. Lastly, the ground is added and the work finished.

A great deal has been said about the necessity of keeping to the character of the lace which is being worked, and never using stitches foreign to its style, which points are very necessary to be observed if an imitation is desired. But the writer would like to offer a word of suggestion on the other side of the subject.

Why imitate the work of a special district ?

Why not make the principles and methods proper to the craft your own—a part of yourself—by study, reflection and practice, as well as by the careful observation of the best work of various times and countries ? Having done this, why not produce, no copy more or less accurate of the lace of a certain time or district, but an expression of yourself through this most artistic medium ?

The lace of any given district probably took its characteristics from idiosyncrasies of teachers and workers and from the exigencies and possibilities of the life around them.  Be content to start your own district with the best that you know and can do, then it is possible that future generations may be agreed that your lace was the most beautiful in all the world : or, if your work must take a lower standard, you will still be likely to give people what they dearly love—a little change.

Good lace, like good jewellery, should be an heirloom.  Do not, then, make nets with coarse meshes simply because they are quicker to work.  A little weariness will be forgotten to-morrow, or only remembered with pride ; but poor work will annoy its maker as long as the lace will last.  A well-finished piece of work is a solid satisfaction, worth a little fag, repaying the worker for the exercise of some amount of patience.  Consider that your work is for posterity, so making it strong, and uniformly good.

For good lace, only flax thread should be used, cotton loses its shape in washing.

Patterns should be started from the left and the winding of the pattern followed towards the right.

The right side of the lace is next the pillow.

The upper side is used for taking out a knot, or any strengthening work it is desirable to hide.

Before grounding, enough pins must be pushed down to preserve the contour of the work.

All twists should be made from right to left.  Thread is made with a turn from left to right, hence if two threads are twisted with that same turn they will blend and appear too much like one thread.

When coarse thread is used, less twisting is required.

Belgian workers commonly twist twice at edge-making, English ones generally three times.

Bobbins should be firmly and evenly wound, and threads kept as short as convenient for working.

The threads should at no time after winding be touched with the fingers.  If the thread does not run well from the bobbin a needle-pin should be used.

Bobbins should be spread out in the shape of a fan.  The left gimp should touch the pin on that side, and the right one touch the right-hand pin.

In making half stitch, do not omit to cross the weavers after passing the first gimp or else to uncross them before passing the second.  The first way gives the better appearance.

If carrying a lace pillow out of doors, pin an unfolded handkerchief under the bobbins, bringing it up over them, so forming a pocket which must be secured at both ends.  This prevents loss in case of the accidental breaking of a thread.

Cleanliness of the daintiest order should be the constant care of a good worker.  Hands should be frequently washed and large, white cloths or aprons arranged to guard against soil from a dark gown. Bobbins also should be washed before winding if their condition be at all doubtful.

When leaving the work, if it be but for a moment, cover with a fold of the pillow handkerchief. If leaving it for half an hour, pin a piece of wide tape down close to the bobbins and throw a large handkerchief over all, as well as the folded one on the pillow. When definitely putting up, pin the extra handkerchief in place, preventing possible dust.

Beware of kittens.

**Torchon.**—In starting to work any new kind of lace, it is always best to begin with a simple pattern.

Obtain a pricked pattern marked with working lines, and either a small piece of the lace you are about to work or a clear illustration.

Pin the pattern firmly on the pillow, with the straight edge (the footing) to the left. Provide plenty of strong pins and good thread, linen for choice, of the fineness desired. Examine the lace at its widest part ; and count the number of bobbins required. Large bobbins are generally used for this lace, to give room for the rather coarse thread.

The footing will probably take three pairs, for two cords and a pair of weavers to go backwards and forwards.

The heading, which, in Torchon, is an open grille made by half stitch, will want some half dozen pairs : but count them to make sure. Now look at the heading again and count how many little twisted bars come out from it on one side, between its highest and lowest curve. These may be three in a narrow edging. Twelve pairs then will be needed. These may be hung on pins, in suitable holes, in sets of two pairs. It is usual to commence the work where the heading begins to rise, at the lowest point of the scallop. The heading is worked in half stitch. The two cords of the footing are twisted, each two or three times, and the weavers make a whole stitch each time they work with either of them. For the middle of the lace, it is merely a matter of following the pattern. Here may be a Torchon stitch and there a cobweb. Here the scallop is rising and throws out pairs of bobbins with which to work the middle. There it contracts and takes in pair after pair to make a wider heading, which may presently almost reach the footing.

If the method of making the stitches and bars and working the cobwebs, leaves, etc., is known, the rest is merely common sense and observation : the sole difficulty being to throw out from the heading and take in again at the right places the pairs of bobbins used for working the middle.

**Maltese, Guipure, Bedfordshire.**—Like Torchon, the pattern for this should not only be correctly pricked, but marked by lines which may act as guides to the worker.

The characteristic features of this lace are two: a great preponderance of leaf stitch, oval and square, short and long, and winding paths of clothwork made with no open edge. For these paths, the weavers work through the warps, are crossed and return; taking in and throwing out pairs as the pattern requires.

Carelessly made, this lace is most unsatisfactory; but can certainly be made quickly and cheaply, if not so much so as Torchon.

The bobbins used should not be too small, and are generally weighted with ornamental beads. Both footing and heading differ so much in the various patterns that the number of bobbins needed for them cannot be predicted.

Obtaining a piece of lace of the required pattern, or a clear illustration of it, count the number of pairs of bobbins used in it. One pair is used for a twist, two pairs for a plait, three pairs (counting the weavers) for a narrow path and four for one of ordinary width. The widest part of the scallop will be found easiest to count.

Having provided the necessary number of well-wound bobbins, hang the required pairs for the heading, the footing, the paths, etc., on pins at the places where they are wanted. It will probably be found better to start at the narrowest part of the lace.

**Lille, Buckinghamshire, Point, Mechlin.**—When well made, this is a highly satisfactory lace. It is largely made on the Continent, and both Bucks and Beds pride themselves upon the beauty of some very fine patterns. With both English counties it is largely referred to as " Point," which is a most indeterminate name, being used with a prefix for many kinds of net, while Lille net has not so pre-eminent a standing as to claim the unprefixed title.

Before attempting to make any pattern, whatever the class of lace, a piece of that lace, or a clear illustration of it, should be obtained, and also a well-pricked pattern. From the lace, or illustration, count the number of pairs ; and note if and where the thick thread, called gimp, is used. Count the threads that run lengthwise in the heading and footing, and remember that beside these both footing and heading must have weavers and probably edge bobbins ; and finish by numbering the pairs used in the middle.

Having provided as many well-wound bobbins as required, hang them in sets of two pairs, on pins just above the holes for which they will be used, adding a third pair where it will be wanted for weaving.

In working, connection between the heading and the middle net is obtained by throwing out and taking in pairs from or to the heading.

Connection between the footing and the middle is made by stitches between the weavers and the net bobbins.

Spots, or other ornaments, are worked by using the net bobbins bordering the marked places, as warps and weavers as required. Careful observation of the lace sample will show the details.

Note must be taken of the place and manner of weaving the gimps in and out to outline spots, etc.

The methods of working Mechlin are the same as for Lille, with the exception of the number of stitches to each mesh of the net.  But the Belgian workers of both grounds are apt to omit the use of pins in making the net itself.  For Mechlin, it is customary to use exceedingly fine thread, which with the extra stitches in each mesh of the net gives the reason of its high price.

**Valenciennes.**—The directions for this may be taken from those for Lille with a few exceptions.

There is, of course, the characteristic net (p. 87) and the point that the lace should be made with exceedingly fine thread. Then, too, the ordinary footing may be present or may be reduced to a single pair of cord bobbins.  However, the special peculiarity of this lace is the habit of the workers of making a tie between two bobbins when, on bringing in pairs from the meshes into the spots or other ornaments, it is considered necessary to ensure that they shall not pull away from each other. Owing to the bars having four threads, the passage of the weavers and warps from and into them is less easy than with the twisted meshes.

# CHAPTER V

# EDGES

## HOW TO MAKE PICOTS

WHEN picots are made with an open edge on both sides of a braid, the bobbins which form the cord, and which are left one at either side, keep always the same position. Only the pair which make the picots travel backwards and forwards. Or if the picots are on one side only, on that side the cord bobbins keep their place, while the pair which makes the picots travels. Hence the picot-making bobbins are emptied quicker than the

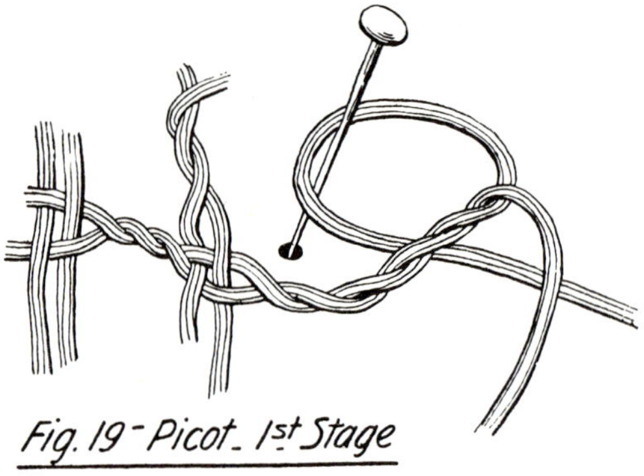

Fig. 19 - Picot - 1st Stage

others, and it is well sometimes, after the picot is made, to change places with a cord bobbin, which may have a larger store of thread; the one crossing necessary will not be likely to show.

To make picots with an open edge, work the weavers through the warps, twist, and make the stitch with the resting bobbins. Now twist the weavers six times, take a pin in the right hand and place its point under the thread of the outside weaver. Form a loop round the pin, by lifting the thread with it and turning it round with its point towards the bobbin, which hangs from the thread. (See Fig. 19.) Place the pin carrying the loop in the next pinhole. Pull the bobbin whose thread is round the pin

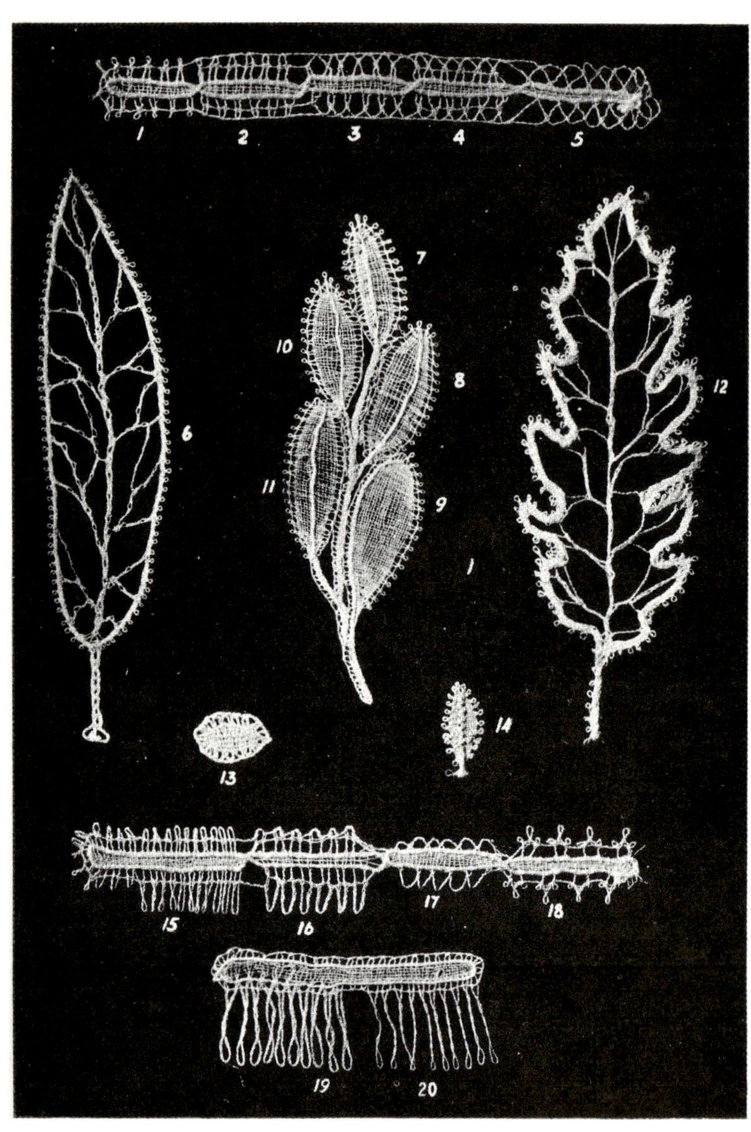

EXAMPLES OF ORDINARY AND NEW METHODS

[face p. 4?

# PLATE I

1. Ordinary edge with picots.
2. Plain double edge.
3. Double edge long loop.
4. Double edge spotted.
5. Double loop edge.
6. Skeleton leaf lace.
7. Raised work.    Linen cord lined.
8.        ,,        ,,      Twisted cord.
9.        ,,        ,,      Stem stitch.
10.      ,,        ,,      Linen cord.
11.      ,,        ,,      Rope stitch.
12. Skeleton leaf lace.
13. Invisible hanging on and unseen finishing.
14. Plaited loops entwined.
15. Twisted fringe.
16. Plaited fringe.
17. Loop edge.
18. Triple picot edge.
19. Plaited fringe.
20. Twisted fringe.

gently, while its comrade is held with its thread a little slack. When the first picot bobbin is pulled, the thread of the second bobbin will show a tendency to follow that of the first round the pin. Make it do so (that will be to pass the thread of the second bobbin round the same pin from the outside, passing the thread between the two last pins). Lay the second bobbin down on the left of the first and cross the first over it. (See Fig. 20.)

This last crossing is not general, but is recommended both for strength and appearance.

Make a stitch. This passes the picot-making bobbins again through the cord-makers, which will be left at the side as usual.

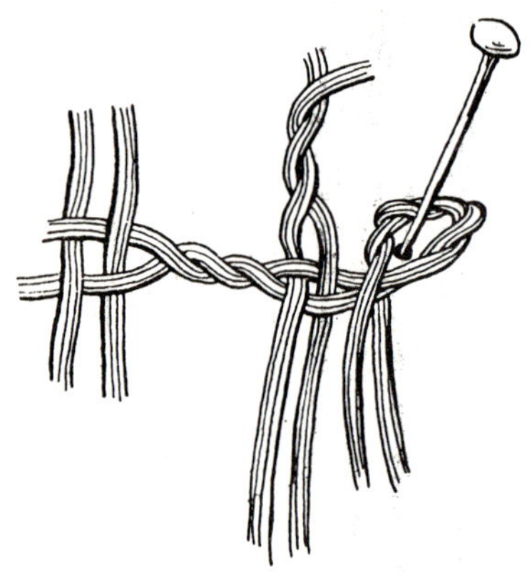

Fig. 20 - Picot - 2nd Stage

Pull the two pairs of bobbins apart, and tighten the stitch against the pin. Twist each pair and work as usual.

When lace is grounded, picots are used for the outer edge only. In ungrounded sprays, etc., they may be effectively used as a finish to leaves, flowers, or other ornaments.

For this purpose, and some others, the picot may have a better appearance without the open edge between it and the clothwork. When so made a pair of the fine-thread bobbins are usually kept outside the gimp to use in completing the picot. This is essential if picots are used as an edge to half stitch, when the gimp must have at least one companion to be worked plainly, either inside or out.

1. **Ordinary Edge; Plain** (p. 21).

2. **Ordinary Edge, with Picots** (p. 44).

3. **Double Edge : Plain.**—The pattern for this should have a double row of pinholes at each side, the second or outer row being at the distance of one pinhole from the next. Each outer pinhole must be in line with the inner.

For this edge two pairs of edge (resting) bobbins are provided for each side on which it is to be worked. (See Fig. 21.)

When the weavers have been worked through the warps twisted and have only the two edge pairs outside them, set a pin in the inner pinhole, with three pairs of bobbins outside it. Make a stitch with the weavers and the inner edge pair and twist the weavers three times, but not the other pair. Set a pin in the outer hole with two pairs of bobbins outside it, make a stitch

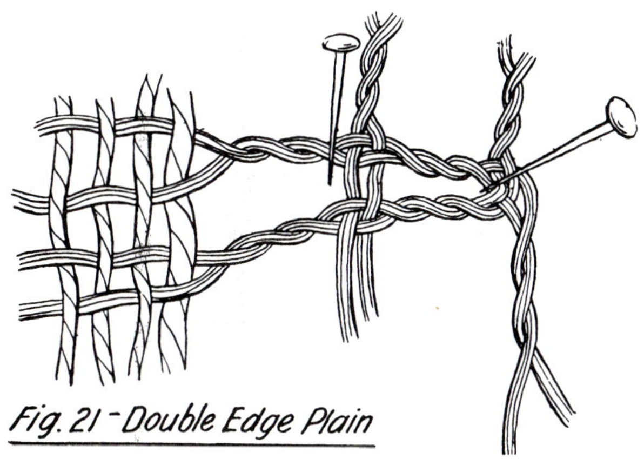
*Fig. 21 - Double Edge Plain*

between the two outer pairs and twist both pairs three times. Leave the outside pair to rest and take the next as weavers, stitching them with the pair lying next the inside pin. Twist both pairs three times and work the weavers across as usual.

4. **Double Edge : Long Loop.**—This pattern must have a double row of pinholes, the second row at the distance outside of one pinhole from the next. The outer pinholes are alternate with the inner.

Two edge pairs of bobbins are necessary for each side where this border is to be worked. (See Fig. 22.)

When the weavers have worked through the warps, have been twisted and have only the two edge pairs outside them, a pin is set in the inner hole, with three pairs of bobbins outside it. Stitch the weavers with the next pair (which should have already been twisted) and twist each pair three times. Set a pin in the outer hole, with two pairs outside it (both with twists), make a stitch between those two pairs, twist them each three times and lay them back.    There will now be three pairs at the edge.    Take the pair next the warps, work through them and repeat.

5. **Double Edge : Spotted.**—The pattern for this is the same as for No. 4.    Three pairs of bobbins are left for the edge, each with three twists.    (See Fig. 23.)

Work the weavers through the warps, twist three times and make a stitch with the inner pair of edge bobbins.    Set a pin in the inner pinhole with four pairs outside it.    Make a stitch between the weavers and the second edge pair : and another between the third and fourth pairs, counting from the edge, twisting

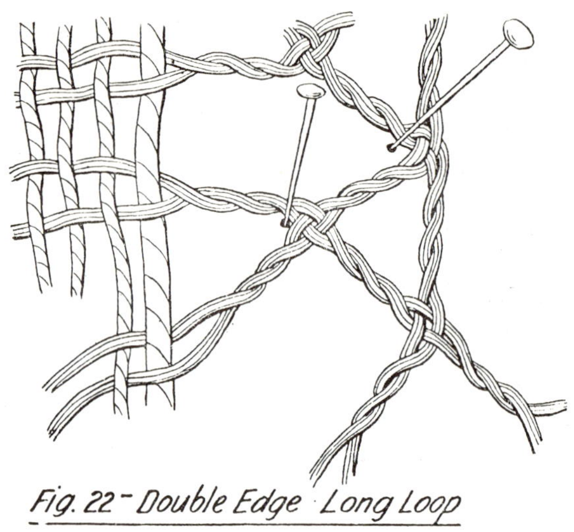

Fig. 22 - Double Edge  Long Loop

both pairs three times.    Set a pin in the outer hole with two pairs outside it.    Twist the weavers three times, make a stitch with the outside pair and twist each pair three times.

Take the fourth pair from the edge for the new weavers ; see that they are twisted and work them on.

6. **Loop Edge.**—This may be worked on an ordinary pattern, or if long or wide loops are wished, or very small close-set ones, alterations must be made as required.

Work the weavers straight through warp and edge bobbins without twisting, and set the pin with only the weavers outside it.    Twist the weavers and lay them down, returning as usual with the inner pair, but without twisting.    (See Fig. 24.)

The twisting is regulated according to the length of loop wished from three to six times or more.

7. **Double Loop Edge.**—The pattern is the same as for No. 4, or a single row of pinholes may be used.

The weavers are worked until there are but two pairs of bobbins

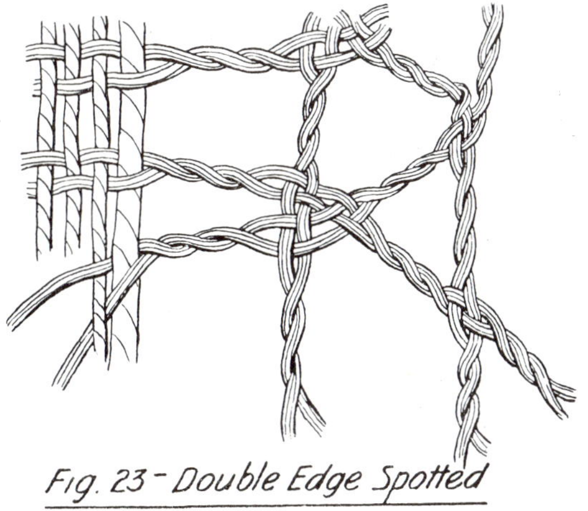

Fig. 23 - Double Edge Spotted

outside them; these are the two pairs which in all double-row edges are required to rest at the side. (See Fig. 25.) Without

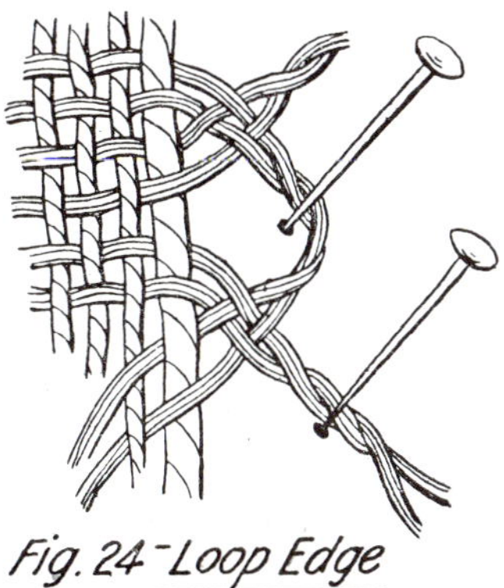

Fig. 24 - Loop Edge

twisting the weavers make a stitch between them and the inner edge pair, which should have three twists; and set a pin inside the two outer pairs in the inner pinhole if this be provided. Now twist the weavers three times and stitch with the outer pair, which should have been six times twisted, and set a pin in the outer pinhole between the two outer pairs. The weavers will now be outside: twist them six times and the next pair three times and lay down both pairs.   Return with the pair next the warps without twisting.   In commencing, note that the pinhole employed must be the one slightly in advance of the crossing, or last hole used.

8. **Triple Picot Edge.**—The pattern for this edge must have the pinholes arranged in triplets with the same space between each triplet as between the pinholes which compose it.   To prepare it draw a line on an ordinary pattern outside the pinholes and at the same distance from them as that between each pair of pinholes.

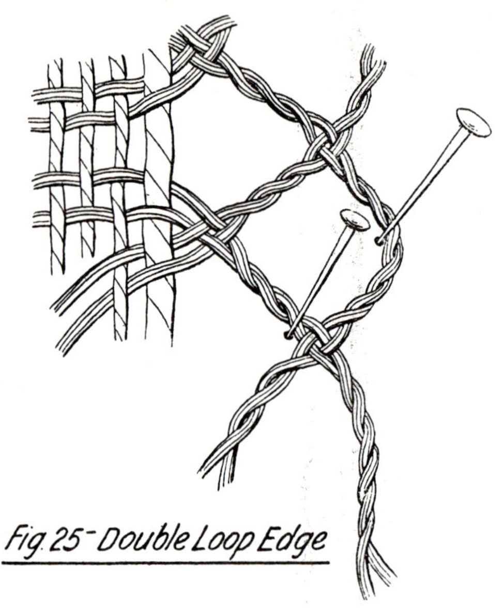

Fig. 25 - Double Loop Edge

Along this line make a pinhole between the first and second holes of the ordinary pattern, then between the third and fourth, etc., leaving the spaces between the second and third, fourth and fifth, etc., free.   This gives a series of triple pinholes.   (See Fig. 26.) For working, as soon as the weavers have worked through the warps and have been twisted they are stitched with the edge pair, the resting weavers.   A picot is now made with the weavers in the first hole on the inner line and completed by a stitch with the edge or resting bobbins, which will make the next picot in the hole on the outer line.   Finish this by a stitch with the weavers and make the third picot with them in the third hole of the triplet.   Finish by a stitch with the edge bobbins, twist both pairs and work the weavers across.   Having made the opposite edge, work the weavers back to the gimp at the space between the triplet last

made and the next one, cross the weavers round the gimp, return
to the opposite gimp and if needful cross the weavers round that

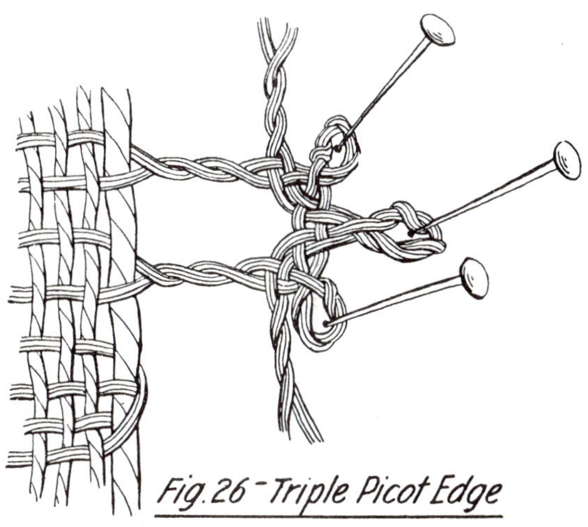

*Fig. 26 – Triple Picot Edge*

gimp also.   Return to the side of the first triplet and make the
next in the same manner.

*Fig. 27 – Twisted Fringe Edge*

The manœuvre of taking the weavers backwards and forwards
between the gimps is done in order that the clothwork may be

well filled up (with no warps showing) and yet enough space left between the triplets for each one to show well.

9. **Twisted Fringe Edge.**—The pattern for this must have a row of holes pricked outside the ordinary edge holes (which should be very close together) and opposite to them at a distance suitable for the width of the fringe which, for fine work, may range from one to three-eighths of an inch.   (See Fig. 27.)

When the weavers have worked through the warps, they are twisted as usual and stitched with the cord bobbins.   They are then twisted a sufficient number of times to make a cord to reach to the first hole, which regulates the width of the fringe and back to the edge.   Only experience can determine the amount of

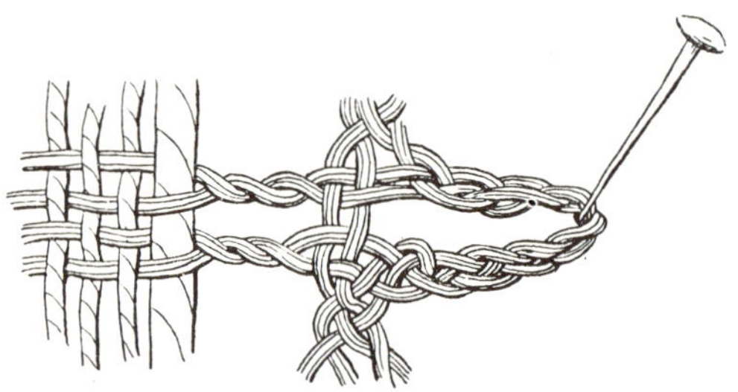

### Fig. 28. Plaited Fringe Edge

twisting required for this, which should combine the threads into a firm even cord, and should cause the loop to form a secondary twist, when the pin is removed, along the whole of its length. Having arranged the loop a stitch is made with the cord bobbins to complete it.   Both pairs are twisted three times, the cord (resting) bobbins are laid back and the inner pair taken as weavers.

10. **Plaited Fringe Edge.**—The pattern is the same as for No. 9. Four edge bobbins must be provided.   (See Fig. 28.)

When the weavers reach the edge, they are twisted three times and worked in half-stitch with the inner edge pair, which is then left.   A plait is then made with the weavers and outer edge pair of a length sufficient to reach round the pin and back to the edge. The inner pair of the plait is now taken for weavers worked in half-stitch with the pair left at the edge twisted and worked across as usual.   The two edge pairs may be half-stitched twice, or each pair twisted three times and either left as they are or the right-hand pair crossed over the left.

# CHAPTER VI

# RAISED WORK

1. **OLD GUIMPE.**—This is merely a bar with the ordinary edge at one side, and stem stitch at the other. It is run up on one side of a leaf, or ornament, to its end ; and overlaid by linenwork covering the leaf and fastened to the bar at its open edge. The number of bobbins used for this differs, but ten is so usual that one name for it in Devon is " ten stick."

Raised work adds greatly to the selling value of the lace, but its artistic merit depends on the workmanship. It should not be stiff, but lend itself easily to the curves of the pattern ; and for this the utmost care must be taken with the tension at the stem-stitch edge. When that curves outwards, the tension should incline to slackness ; but a firmer tension should be used with an inward curve.

Stem stitch itself is simply a half-stitch and a whole stitch made in succession with the same two pairs of bobbins, one pair being the weavers brought through from the open edge and the other the last pair on the opposite side.

As soon as the raised border is worked to the place where a leaf begins to narrow towards its point, an extra pair of bobbins is hung on a pin near the open edge, and stitched with the weavers as soon as they have passed the warps. The weavers are then twisted and stitched with the edge bobbins as usual. The pin holding the bobbins is withdrawn and the extra bobbins pulled up, while the weavers are firmly held. The extra bobbins are then laid on one side, again supported by a pin. (See Fig. 29.)

This is repeated before each pinhole until only one pinhole before that at the tip of the leaf is left. After a pin has been set in this the returning weavers are twisted three times as usual, stitched with the first pair of warp bobbins and laid over the part just made : ready to be used when the pillow is turned. The pair outside on the stem-stitch edge are taken as weavers, worked through and the edge made with them. The pin is set in the tip of the leaf, and the weavers are twisted and make a stitch with the next pair of warps, after which they are laid back as before. The pair now outside on the stem-stitch side are taken as weavers worked through, and the edge made with them, the pin being set in the first hole on the further side of the tip. (See Fig. 30.) The pillow is now turned and the last pair of warps put with the two pairs just laid back.　The whole leaf is now worked across from side to side.

The returning weavers are stitched first with the only remaining pair of warps, then with the pair hanging below the pin at the

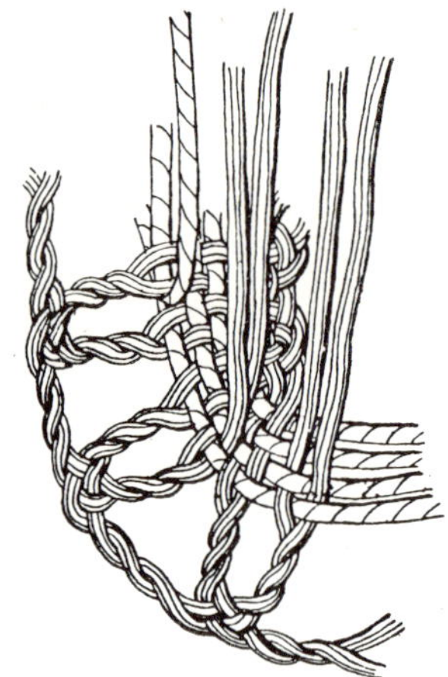

*Fig. 29 - Raised work Turning 1st Stage*

point, and next with the pair against the neighbouring pin.　With the latter pair a stem or turning stitch is made, the outer pair laid down and the next ones taken for the return.

*Fig. 30 - Raised work Turning 2nd Stage*

This method is used for each row where bobbins were left.　If the work should widen suddenly so that extra bobbins are needed, they may be added under cover of the guimpe or where the appearance of the work will be improved by them.

When all the bobbins have been picked up and used, at every

row a sewing must be made to one of the cords of the nearest loop of the open edge, close to the clothwork.

In working a branch of leaves, it is usual to start from the end of the stem either in double-stem stitch or guimpe, using extra bobbins for the lower part if preferred and throwing them off later by degrees. The stem is run to the top leaf and that is worked first. Then another narrower stem is run and sewn either on the top of, or beside, the one already made. This runs to the next leaf. From this when finished another stem is run to the next leaf and so on till the branch is completed.

Another method is to work the lower leaves in succession as the stem is brought to their level.

The raised work may be run up each leaf as a mid-rib instead of at the edge, with good effect if well and lightly made : but it must be neither stiff nor heavy. Raised work should have an appearance both dainty and rich.

2. **Rope.**—This is so often made in a careless, or even slovenly, way that a good teacher is often afraid to recommend it, unless a student is deliberately making inferior lace.

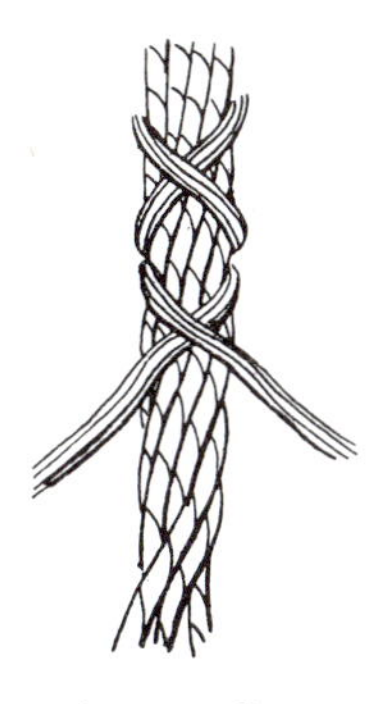

The rope even well made is quicker to work than the guimpe and its object is the same. It enables the worker to reach the point of a leaf, etc., from its opposite extremity in a strong and neat manner, without the delay of cutting off and restarting.

It may also be used to cross work already made ; when it must run in places where it will show least, and be kept in position by a sufficient number of sewings. For this, being on the wrong side, it will not need an elaborate finish, but is better made loosely, to lie as flat as may be. (See Fig. 31.)

The raised rope as made in Brussels and Bruges is started by tying each pair of bobbins once, with an extra tie to one pair

Fig. 31–Rope

selected for binding, which are then opened out. The rest of the bobbins are gathered up, twisted from right to left and laid between the pair reserved for binding, which are then passed over and under the bundle of threads, crossing each other's thread above and below. The binding should be even, and the crossings exactly one below the other and fairly close together. When the length required is completed, the binders are firmly tied and the rope fixed in place with pins.

To start making a leaf when the rope is fixed just beneath its point, two pairs are taken from the rope bobbins and each twisted three times. Set a pin in the hole at the point and lay the twisted pairs one on each side of it. Make a stitch with them

behind the pin and twist each pair three times.  Lay each pair
on its own side and take another pair from the rope bobbins,
twisting them three times and making a stitch with the pair laid
on the left side.   Set a pin in the next hole on the left of the point,
with the two pairs just stitched outside it.  Twist both pairs
three times and lay the outside pair back, taking the inner pair
as weavers.  Work across to the other side, using four pairs from
the rope bobbins as warps.  If more bobbins be left, pick them up
as the weavers pass the rope.  If the number of pairs of rope
bobbins were less than seven, more could have been added under
cover of the rope, and extra pairs may be taken in that way as
the work widens.

Sewings must be made into the rope at least every second or
third row.

3.  **Cord.**—This is, the writer believes, new.  At all events she
has not come across it anywhere.  It is simple and effective, and
made with few, or many, bobbins, according
to the style of lace in hand.   (See Fig. 32.)

The collected bobbins are bound round by
one of their pairs and tied.  Then divide them
into two equal groups, straightening their
threads and making them of equal length, say
3 to 4 in. Each division is then twisted from
right to left evenly throughout its length.
Then the two divisions are twisted round
each other, from left to right, until a handsome cord is formed of the length required,
when it is firmly pinned into place, the pins
being driven through both cords.

The rest of the work is the same as for the
Rope (p. 55).

4A.  **Linen-stitch Cord.**—There is no need
for preliminary tying with this cord.  (See
Fig. 33.)

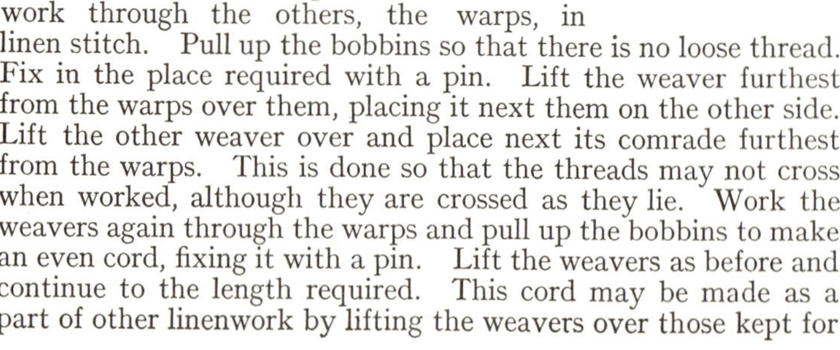

Fig. 32 Cord

Lay the bobbins out evenly as for ordinary
clothwork.  Take one pair as weavers and
work through the others, the warps, in
linen stitch.   Pull up the bobbins so that there is no loose thread.
Fix in the place required with a pin.  Lift the weaver furthest
from the warps over them, placing it next them on the other side.
Lift the other weaver over and place next its comrade furthest
from the warps.   This is done so that the threads may not cross
when worked, although they are crossed as they lie.  Work the
weavers again through the warps and pull up the bobbins to make
an even cord, fixing it with a pin.   Lift the weavers as before and
continue to the length required.   This cord may be made as a
part of other linenwork by lifting the weavers over those kept for

the cord, working through the cord bobbins, pulling up the cord and weavers carefully and then lifting the weavers back over the cord warps to continue their journey to the other side. When the weavers have made the edge, they must be pulled gently and the row adjusted. The return row will be worked in the same way, the cord being always worked backwards, the weavers being always lifted over it before and after it is worked.

The writer believes this cord to be new. It is very strong :

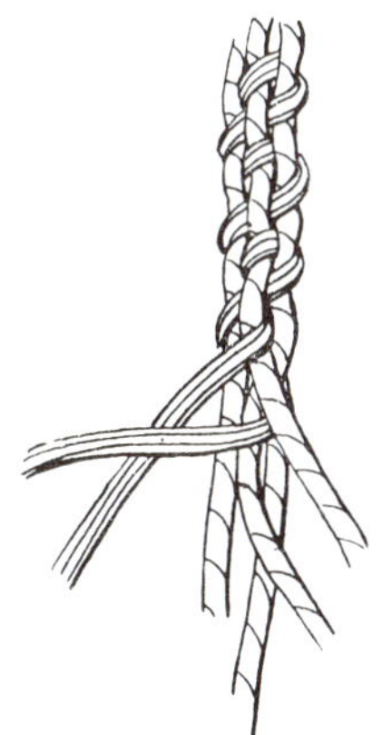

Fig. 33—Linen-stitch Cord

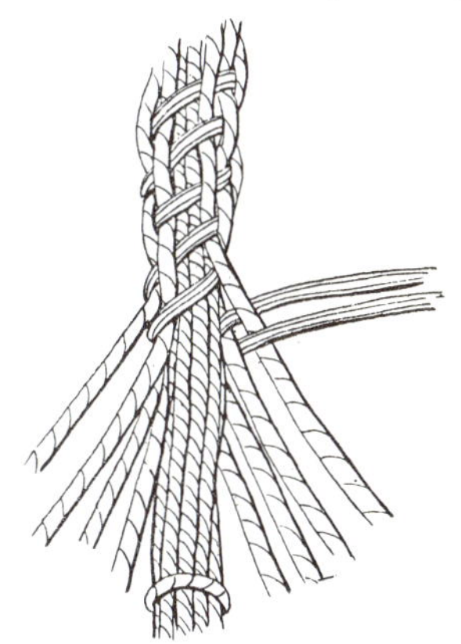

Fig. 34—Linen-stitch Cord lined

and well worked has, perhaps, a better appearance than any of the others. If wanted of larger size than that made by three pairs of warps, No. 4B will be found the better method.

4B. **Linen-stitch Cord: Lined.**—This is the same as No. 4A, but worked round a core of threads.

If four pairs of bobbins are to be used for the outer covering, provide three pairs for the lining. These are hung to an edge or where required and their threads tied round near the bobbins to distinguish them from the warps and keep them straight. Two pairs of warps are hung on their right, two on their left, and the weavers outside all. (See Fig. 34.)

Work the weavers through the two nearest pairs of warps, pass them under the tied bobbins, work through the other warps and pull warps and weavers up carefully. Lift the foremost weaver back to the side it started from, and lay it next the warps. Lift over the second weaver, lay next the first, and work the weavers through, passing them under the tied bobbins, when they are reached as before. Pull up again, lift over the weavers and continue to the length required.

5. **Corona.**—The linenwork in this being double, extra bobbins must be provided, their number depending on the width deter-

mined for the corona ; the position of these, for a border corona, being at one side with one pair of warps outside them. It is better to make the corona on one side only at first to gain a clear knowledge of the working. (See Fig. 35.)

After the edge has been made on the side on which the corona is arranged, and the weavers have been twisted, work through to the end of the extra bobbins, make a stem stitch and leave the weavers with the corona bobbins.

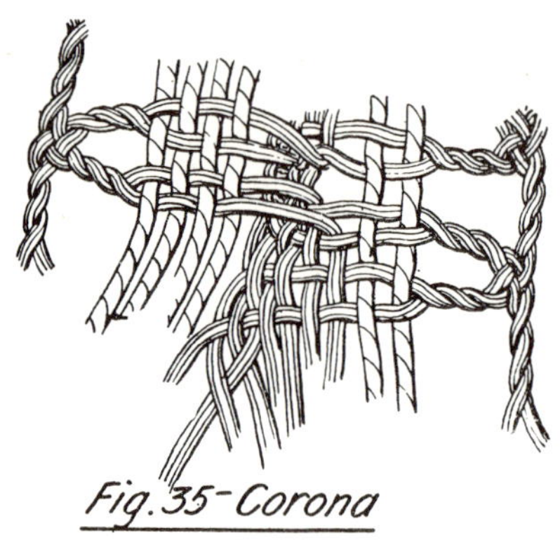

Fig. 35 - Corona

If there be three pairs of these, number three pairs, counting the weavers as one pair and put a pin on either side of them, standing well up, to divide them from the other bobbins. As the weavers have been counted as belonging to the corona, one of the extra pairs will be left outside the pin. Take these for weavers ; they will be third and fourth from the edge. Pass the third over the fourth so that their position is reversed (if this were not done there would be a twist in the clothwork) and lift them over the extra bobbins, which rest now till the next row.

Work the weavers through to the further edge, which will be made as usual. The return journey is also as usual until the extra bobbins are reached, when the weavers are lifted over them and laid next their boundary pin, the foremost bobbin being lifted first and laid next the pin, with the other beside it. Take the second pair of corona bobbins counting from the stem stitch border and work them through the others to the edge, which is made as usual. Return as in the first row to the end of the coronas and make a stem stitch, leaving the weavers as in the first row. Before working the corona the boundary pin on that side should be removed. The work is continued in the same manner, counting the coronas, taking the next pair as weavers, lifting them over the coronas, working them to the further side and returning as before. The writer believes this work to be new.

# CHAPTER VII

# ORNAMENTAL CLOTHWORK

I. **HALF-STITCH.**—At first this title seems a misnomer, for the thing it denotes is really three-quarters of a cloth stitch ; but further consideration brings to mind the fact that the name was given by the workers of net-grounded laces, who frequently make one of these stitches, set a pin and complete with another of them, which gives a natural reason for the name.

The Belgians call two half-stitches following each other as above a " passée double " (or double stitch) and a single one a " demi-passée " : so our " half-stitch " may be a simple translation.

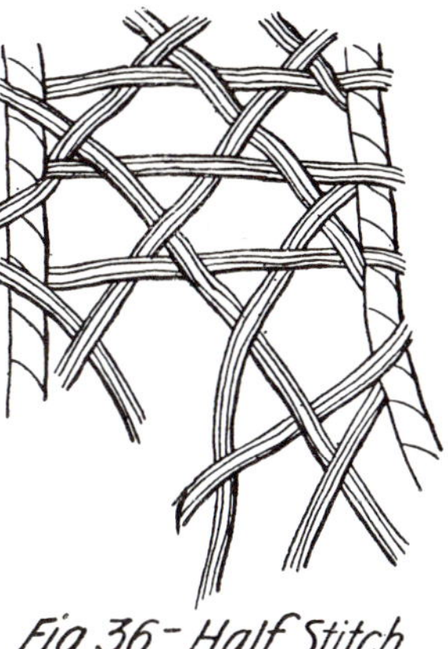

Fig. 36 - Half Stitch

Repeated rows of this stitch form a pretty open-work material of a texture between muslin and net : while isolated stitches are used to draw threads together and for other purposes connected with strength and finish of appearance. (See Fig. 36.)

As in cloth stitch, two pairs of bobbins are used. The movements are the same as the first three of the cloth stitch :—

   1st left   over right with the middle pair.
   2nd right  ,,   left   ,,   ,,   left    ,,
   3rd   ,,   ,,   ,,   ,,   ,,   right   ,,

The movement which in the cloth stitch is fourth, is, in half-stitch, omitted, and, consequently, instead of both weavers passing through the warps, only the foremost passes, while the second is exchanged at each stitch.

Let *ABCD* represent the bobbins as they lie ready to commence. Then the movements are :—

       1st *ACBD*.
       2nd *CABD*.
       3rd *CADB*.

## PLATE II

1. Moss lace.
2. Satin lace.
3. Cross lace.
4. } Leaf stitch on
5. } clothwork.
6. Insertion of leaf stitch.
7. Weavers stitched and Warps stitched.
8. Weavers twisted and Warps stitched.
9. Weavers plain and Warps stitched.
10. Centre perforations.
11. Weavers plain. Warps alternate.
12. Weavers alternate. Warps twisted.
13. Weavers twisted. Warps twisted.
14. Weavers plain. Warps twisted.
15. Half-stitch.
16. Weavers alternate. Warps alternate.
17. Weavers twisted. Warps alternate.
18. Centre twists. Single.
19. Centre twists. Triple.
20. Centre loops.
21. Weavers plain. Warps twisted.
22. Weavers twisted. Warps plain.
23. Seven movement stitch.
24. }
25. } Twisted lines.
26. Centre cobwebs, 4 strands.
27. ,, ,, 6 ,,
28. ,, ,, 8 ,,
29. Centre twists crossed.
30. Ordinary edge.
31. Picot edge.
32. Ordinary edge with picots.
33. Triple picot edge.
34. Plain double edge.
35. Cross stitch.
36. Satin stitch.
37. Moss lace.
38. }
39. } Twisted lace.
40. }
41. Double set leaf and cross.
42. Double set leaf and duplicate trellis.
43. Double set leaf and trellis.
44. Double set chequered leaf.
45. 8-strand (plaited) cobweb with coronet and picots.
46. Chequered leaf.
47. Crossed chequers.
48. Leaves and crosses.
49. Double set leaf and flowers.
50. Cobweb with cross strand.

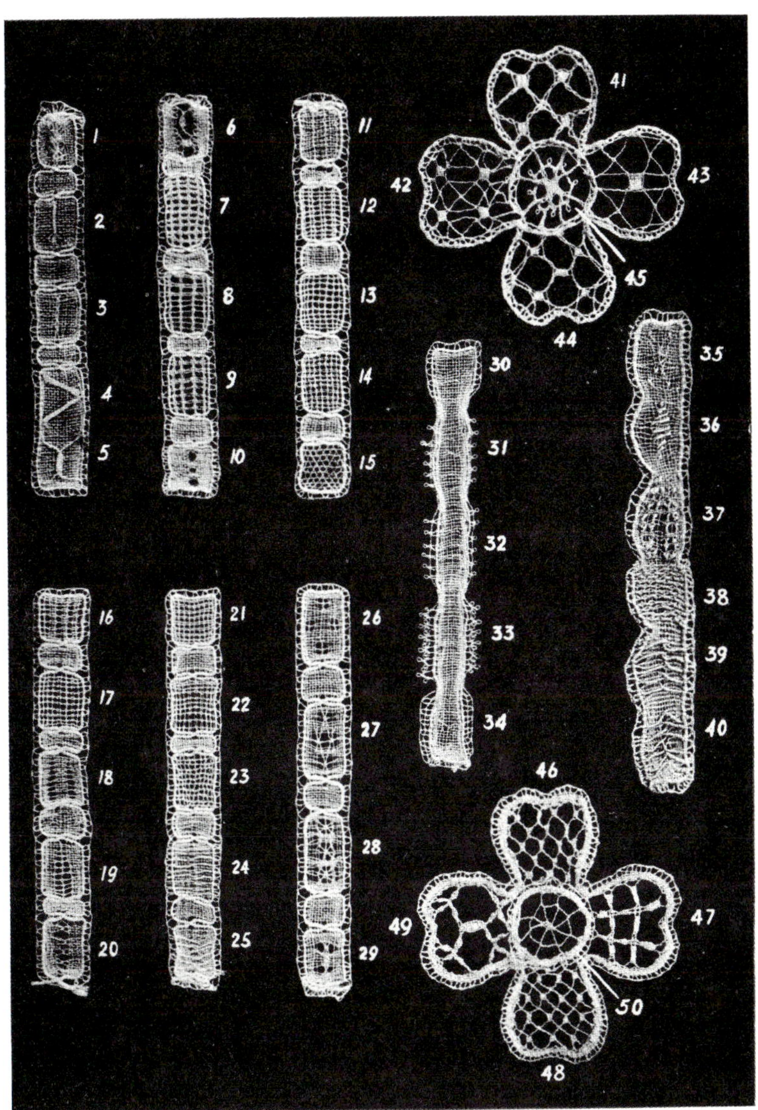

SPECIMENS OF OLD AND NEW STITCHES

Call the next pair of warps $EF$ and the next stitch will be :—

       1st movement $DEBF$.
       2nd    ,,     $EDBF$.
       3rd    ,,     $EDFB$.

Originally $AB$ were the weavers, but $A$ was left behind in the first stitch, $D$ taking its place, which in the second stitch was exchanged with $F$. It is these changes which give character to the stitch.

If gimps are not used with half-stitch, one pair of warps on each side must be worked in plain cloth stitch. The gimp must never be used to make half-stitch, but is passed under one weaver and over the other, before the half-stitch is commenced, and after it is finished. The reason of this is that, as we saw above, half-stitch disturbs the order of the bobbins ; and it is essential that the gimp shall keep its place.

Fig. 37—Weavers Plain Warps Twisted

After passing the first gimp, cross the weavers before the first half-stitch ; or if preferred, uncross them at the end of the row, before passing the second gimp. This is done to make both edges alike. After passing the gimp the bobbins are not crossed (unless purposely), whereas half-stitch always leaves both pairs crossed.

In commencing a cloth of half-stitch, it is usual to cross each pair of warps (from right to left) before making the first stitch.

### $A$. Weavers Plain. Warps Twisted

2. **Single Twists.**—Cross every pair of warps once, from right to left, leaving the gimps, the thick threads, untouched. Then work the weavers across in linen stitch, make the edge, cross the warps and work the weavers back. (See Fig. 37.)

Further rows are a repetition of the same.

### *B.* WEAVERS PLAIN.  WARPS ALTERNATE

For this the number of pairs of warps, not counting the gimps, should be odd, that both edges of the clothwork may correspond.

In working, cross the first pair of warps and leave the next pair plain, and continue this alternation throughout the row.   The

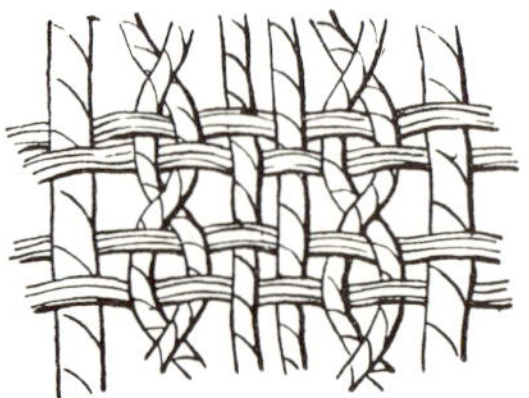

Fig. 38 — Weavers Plain Warps Alternate

weavers are kept plain and the method otherwise as in No. 2A (See Fig. 38.)

It may be varied by leaving the first pair of warps plain and crossing the second pair, and so on alternately.

Another variation is to make the first row begin with crossed warps and the second with plain : thus alternating the rows.

### *C.* WEAVERS TWISTED.  WARPS TWISTED

Like No. 2A, the warps are all crossed ;  but in this the weavers are also crossed, from right to left, before stitching with each pair

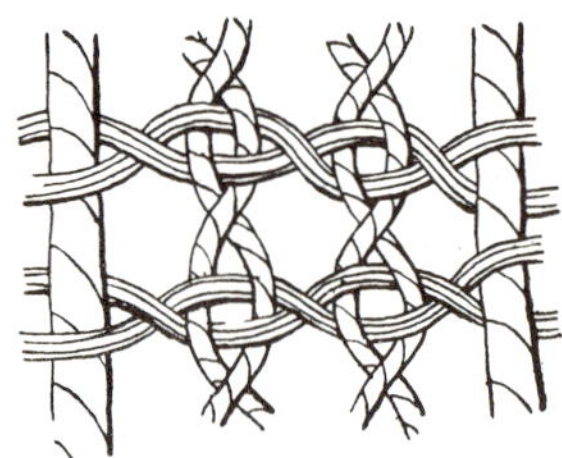

Fig. 39 — Weavers Twisted Warps Twisted

of warps and after using the last warps before the second gimp. Both gimps are passed through the weavers singly, over the thread that lies above and under the one beneath.   (See Fig. 39.)

### *D.* WEAVERS TWISTED.  WARPS ALTERNATE

In this the weavers are as in No. 2C and the warps as in No.

2*B*.   The directions in *B* and *C* will give the method.   (See Fig. 40.)

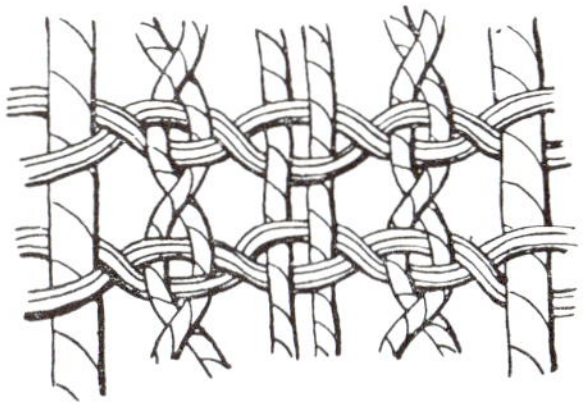

*Fig. 40 - Weavers Twisted Warps Alternate*

### E. WEAVERS TWISTED.   WARPS PLAIN

In this the weavers are treated as in *C* and the warps are left plain.   (See Fig. 41.)

*Fig. 41 - Weavers Twisted Warps Plain*

### F. WEAVERS ALTERNATE.   WARPS TWISTED

The first row of this is worked from the directions for *A* and the second from *C*, further rows being alternately the same.   Or

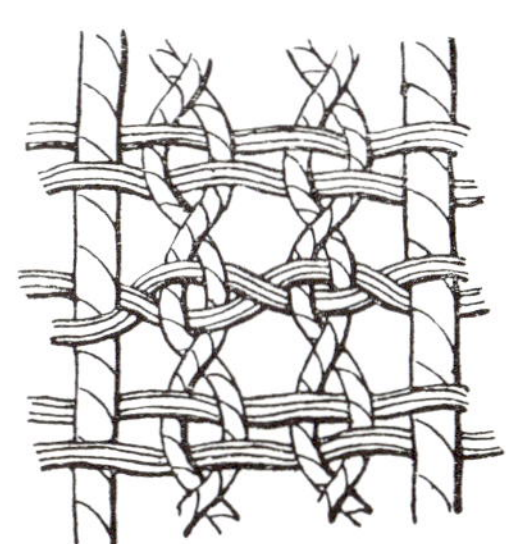

*Fig. 42 - Weavers Alternate Warps Twisted*

the weavers in each row may be alternately twisted and left plain.   (See Fig. 42.)

### *G*. Weavers Alternate. Warps Alternate

In this the weavers are plain in one row and twisted in the next : or in each row alternately twisted and plain: as in *F*. The warps are worked as in *B*.   (See Fig. 43.)

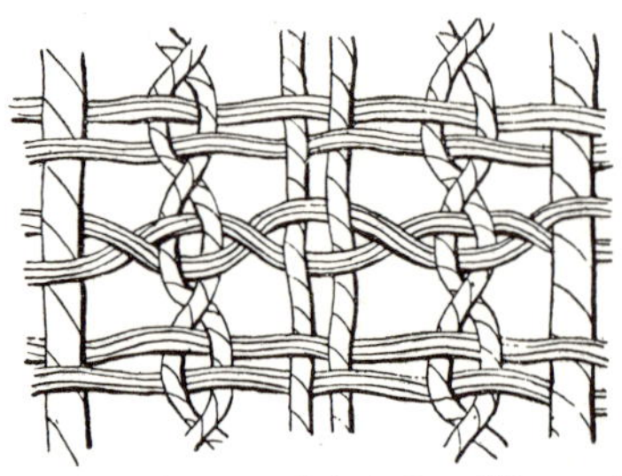

Fig. 43 - Weavers Alternate Warps Alternate

### *H*. Weavers Alternate. Warps Plain

The directions for the weavers may be taken from *G*, while the warps are left plain.   (See Fig. 44.)

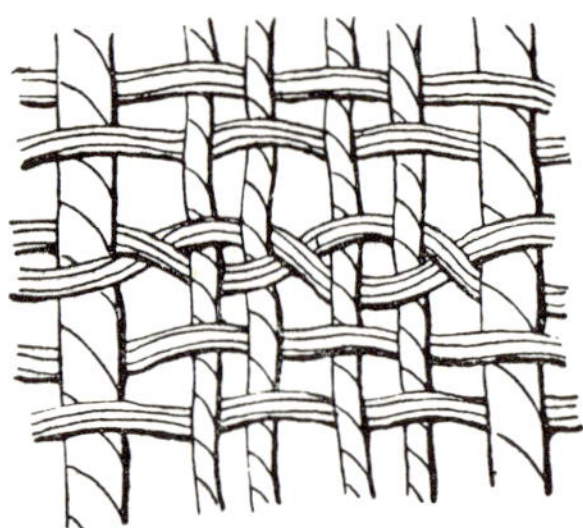

Fig. 44 - Weavers Alternate Warps Plain

3. **Centre Twists : Single.**—This method is useful to mark the veining of a leaf, or to form any geometrical ornamentation upon clothwork.

The pattern should be marked, either by a line or by pinholes, in the place where the twist is wished.   When the weavers reach the mark, twist them once or more as required.   A pin may be set before the next stitch, but is not essential.   (See Fig. 45.)

For veining a leaf, twist once for a few rows nearest the point, then twice for a longer space, and finally three times for the part next the stalk.   This gives a natural widening.

4. **Centre Twists : Triple.**—This is useful for the same purposes as in No. 3.   In working, a twist is given to the warps lying on the mark and to the pairs right and left of them.

The weavers are worked plainly through the first twisted pair,

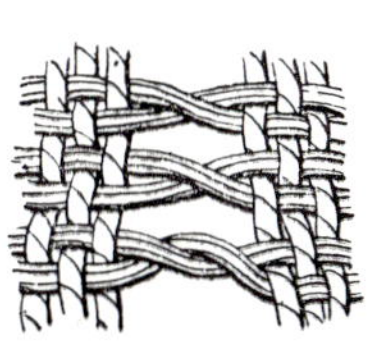

Fig. 45 - Centre Twists Single

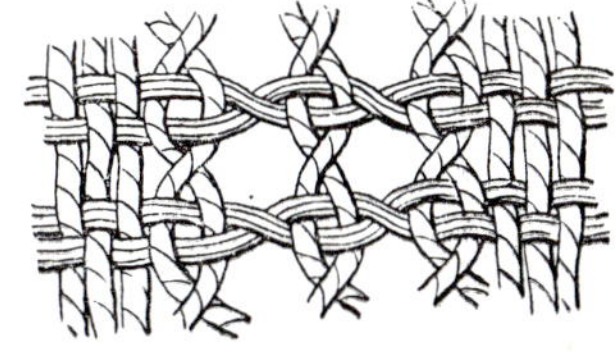

Fig. 46 - Centre Twists Triple

then crossed once or more, worked through the centre twist, crossed as before and worked on.   A pin may be set or not as desired.   (See Fig. 46.)

For a graduated effect, the pair of warps at the mark only are twisted for some rows.   Then for a few rows the weavers are crossed once as well, before and after working the twisted warps.   Next the warp pairs on either side are also twisted ; and

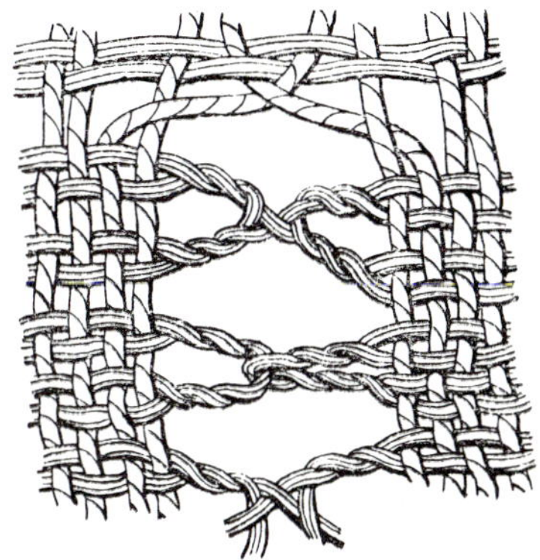

Fig. 47 - Centre Loops Two Methods

then the number of twists given to the weavers may also be increased.

5. **Centre Loops.**—When working a wide leaf or other ornament it is sometimes convenient to divide the bobbins in two sets, each to have its own weaver.

For this a double row of pinholes is provided in the middle, each pair on the same level.   The sides are worked alternately. (See Fig. 47.)

Having divided the bobbins into the two sets, one pair is taken from each set, in the centre, is worked in half-stitch and put back each to the division nearest which they lie. This half-stitch keeps the threads in the middle from slipping as an effect of the division, and should be carefully pulled up. Work a pair of bobbins through the outside pair of warps of the division which has no weavers, or hang them on the gimp. Twist them and make the edge; being careful not to pull the bobbins on which they hang out of place. Work across to the centre; twist the weavers and set a pin in the upper hole on that side with the weavers outside it. Work the weavers of the other division across, twist and set a pin with the weavers outside it.

The two pairs of weavers will now lie side by side, make a half- or linen-stitch between them (the half has some advantages), and return each pair, twisted, to its own division. Or, having twisted each pair of weavers six times, pass the right-hand pair under the left and back to its place. This catches one loop within the other and has perhaps the most finished appearance.

This may be repeated each time the weavers are brought into the centre : or the weavers of both divisions may make a stem stitch with the centre warps and return without touching each other for one or two rows, after which the loops would be repeated.

If the centre loops are discontinued before the end of the leaf, work the spare weavers to their gimp and leave them inside it. Then make a half-stitch between the two centre pairs of warps, pull them up carefully and work the weavers first in use backwards and forwards as usual.

6. **Centre Holes.**—Like No. 5, these holes are worked by separating the bobbins into two divisions, working a half-stitch between the centre pairs, one from each division, and hanging a pair of weavers at the outside edge of that division which has none.

When the weavers reach the centre edge of their division they are worked in stem stitch with the last pair of warps on that side, the return being made with the pair second from the edge after the completion of the stem stitch.

Fig. 48 - Centre Holes

The number of rows worked by each division must be equal. (See Fig. 48.)

When the hole is large enough another half-stitch is worked between the two centre pairs, one from each division. The extra pair of weavers should make the edge even with that finished by the other weavers ; and after twisting should work through the first pair of warps and be laid aside until again required. They would then be twisted a few times, worked through the first pair of warps and used to make the edge and work their division as before. The holes may be graduated or alternated in size with good effect.

### *A*. WEAVERS PLAIN. WARPS STITCHED

**7. Group Stitches.**—The number of warps, not counting gimps, must be divisible by four.

A cloth stitch is made with the first four warps inside the gimp and the bobbins laid down. This is repeated with each set of four in the row.

The weavers are now worked across, and, if two rows between are wished, return to the side from which they started. (See Fig. 49.)

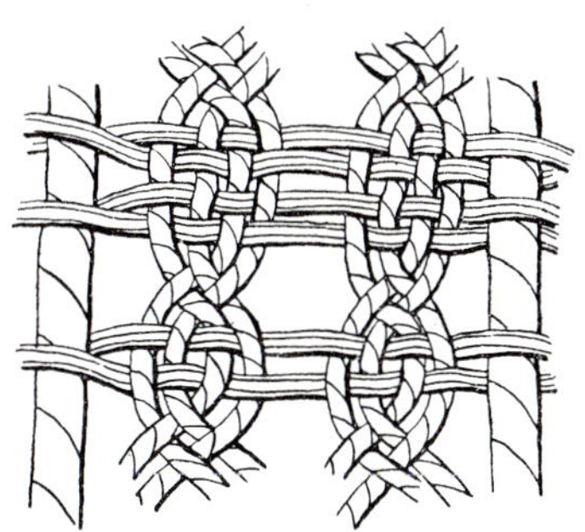

Fig. 49 – Weavers Plain Warps Stitched

After the weavers have worked their one or two rows, the warps are stitched as at first, and the alternate rows of plain work and stitched warps continued.

The gimps are passed through the weavers separately.

### *B*. WEAVERS TWISTED. WARPS STITCHED

The warps are stitched as in *A* ; but, in the second row, the weavers are twisted from once to three times after passing the gimp and after they have worked through the first set of stitched warps, and afterwards between each set and its succeeding one. Either one or two rows may be made by the weavers between each row of stitched warps. Each gimp is passed separately through the weavers. (See Fig. 50.)

### C. Weavers Stitched. Warps Stitched

As for *A* and *B* the warps must be divisible by four.  A double
set of weavers must be provided, viz. the usual edge pairs, two on

*Fig. 50 - Weavers Twisted Warps Stitched*

one side and one on the other ; with an extra pair just inside the
gimp on the side where the two pairs lie outside.  (See Fig. 51.)
Make stitches with each set of warps as in *A ;* leaving the extra
weavers untouched.
Work the edge with the outside weavers and pass the returning
pair through the gimp, work through the extra pair with them
and lay them down.  Pass the extra pair through the gimp, twist
them, put in another pin and make a second edge loop with them.
Pass them through the gimp again and take the two pairs with
which you made the edge for the double set of weavers for the row.

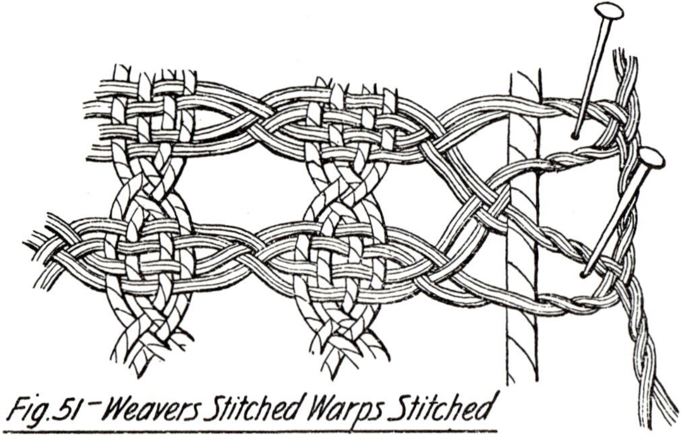

*Fig. 51 - Weavers Stitched Warps Stitched*

Make a stitch with the four weavers, work both pairs through
the next four warps and again stitch the weavers, repeating
alternately till the other gimp is reached, ending with a stitch with
the weavers.  With the first pair of weavers pass the gimp, make

the edge, pass the gimp again and work through the second pair of weavers. Pass the gimp and make the edge with the second weavers, pass the gimp again and make a stitch with the two pairs of weavers. Make a stitch with each set of warps, work the weavers through them and alternately stitch them together and work them through the next set of warps till the gimp is reached. Each row is a repetition of the last.

8. **Insertion of Leaves.**—This makes a pretty footing braid, and is much imitated in machine-made work.

The bobbins are put on in two sets, each with its own warps and three pairs of weavers.

The width of the pattern may be varied to taste, but must have four rows of pinholes.

Arrange each set with one pair of edge bobbins at the outside and two where the two sets meet. Twist the inside weavers three times, stitch them, twist again and work the weavers across. Make each outside edge, work each pair of weavers through the warps, twist them, and lay them down if the leaf is to be short. If a longer leaf is to be made, a pin is set in the inner row with the weavers passed round it, the weavers being then worked to the outside edge and back before being laid down.

To make the leaf, use the inner pairs of side bobbins, twist each pair once or more, make a leaf of the shape preferred (p. 101), twist as at first, and stitch with the weavers. Set a pin in the next inner hole of each division, twist and work across. When the weavers return and are twisted another leaf may be made at once or a pin may be set with the weavers outside it. They are then worked to the outer edge and back before the next leaf is made. This gives an inside pinhole between each two leaves, and has a lighter appearance but less strength.

9. **Leaves on Clothwork.**—The work is started in plain linen stitch and continued to the place where the leaf is desired.

Two pairs of " leaf bobbins " are now prepared by twisting their threads together, and hung between the warps at the places arranged.

If the leaf is desired to lie down the centre of the work, the leaf bobbins should be placed with a pair of them on either side of one, two or three pairs of warps at the centre, each pair of leaf bobbins being supported at its place by a pin.

The warps are lifted and laid on either side out of the way of the leaf bobbins. Each pair of these is now twisted and a leaf of the required length made (p. 101). The pairs are twisted again and laid on one side : the warps being lifted over them and placed ready to start the linenwork, which is continued to the length of the leaf.

The two pairs of leaf bobbins are now slipped under the warps and brought through separately to the upper side of the work in the same places in regard to the centre warps that they were passed through before. The leaf bobbins are then twisted, again stitched, and either twisted and laid aside till wanted anew or tied and cut off.

10. **Embroidery : Cross Stitch.**—Provide an uneven number of warp pairs, counting the gimps. The pairs of weavers are as usual, but an extra pair of bobbins will be needed for the cross stitch. For learning, these may well carry coloured thread, but even an expert will be wise to have them distinctive.

These directions are for a line of cross stitches down the centre of the work.

Support the thread of the cross-stitch bobbins on a pin, and lay one on each side of the centre pair of warps. Work the weavers through till they reach the nearest cross-stitch bobbin. Lift them over it and stitch them with the centre pair. Lift the weavers over the second cross-stitch bobbin and work to the edge. Before the next row, take the left-hand cross bobbin and pass it under the centre pair. Then pass the right-hand cross bobbin under the other cross bobbin and the centre pair. Remove the supporting pin and pull up both cross bobbins gently till the loop which was round the pin has disappeared, but without dragging the threads.

Take the weavers and work the next row, passing them under the cross bobbins.

The third row will be like the first and the fourth like the second. In crossing, the left or right bobbin may be moved first, as preferred, but whichever way is chosen must be strictly adhered to.

Any pattern may be worked in this stitch, a pair of extra bobbins being provided for each additional cross stitch in the same row. The cross-stitch bobbins may be moved about as required on the upper side of the clothwork, which is, as will be remembered, the wrong side ; and are laid left and right of any threads on which it is wished to make a cross stitch.

The cross-stitch bobbins must never be touched by the weavers.

11. **Embroidery : Satin Stitch.**—One or more extra pairs of bobbins will be required for the satin stitch and, for the learner, are better with coloured thread. In any case they should be distinctly marked.

Like No. 10, the pairs of warps are uneven in number, counting the gimps, as these directions are for a line of stitches down the centre of the work.

Hang a pair of embroidering bobbins over a pin ; put one aside and lay the other on the right of the middle pair of warps. Work the weavers across, passing them over the embroidering bobbin. Then pass the latter under the centre pair of warps (bringing it through on their left, between them and the next bobbin) and lay it on one side. Lay the other embroidering bobbin on the right of the centre warps, and work the weavers across again, lifting them over the embroidering bobbin. Pass the second embroidering bobbin under the centre warps, bringing it up as before on their left and laying it aside. Take out the supporting pin and carefully pull up its loop till it disappears. Take the first embroidery bobbin and without crossing its thread over the second lay it on the right of the centre pair of warps, afterwards working the weavers across and continuing in the same manner. If the embroidery stitches are to be closely set, pass the weavers singly through the warps, changing the embroidery bobbins each time a weaver passes.

At no time must the weavers stitch with the embroidering bobbins. The latter must be continually and carefully pulled up, so that their threads are not slack yet do not drag the warps.

An extra pair of bobbins will be required for each satin stitch worked along the row over which the weavers travel.

If the weavers or warps pass over a thread it is left on the right side of the lace : if they are passed under it, it is brought to the upper or wrong side.

12. **Moss.**—This is new, and appears to have great possibilities.

As in the embroidered laces, an extra pair of bobbins is placed where the decoration is arranged. One pair may be in the centre, with one or more pairs on either side, each separated from the others by a pair of warps.

Hang the moss bobbins from a pin and lay them in place. Pass another pair of extra bobbins over and under a gimp, work through the moss bobbins, and pass over and under the other gimp. Lay the extra bobbins back and support each gimp with a pin. Lay a long thin pin under the warps and across the threads of the moss bobbins, from side to side, to keep their loops even. For fine lace the loops may be scarcely longer than the thickness of the pin. This pin must be supported underneath by other pins, at head and point, to keep it from dropping, and two more above at the same places to prevent the loop from being pulled too close to the work.

The pin supporting the moss bobbins is then removed, the loop made by it carefully pulled up, and the moss bobbins laid back, either plain or twisted. The gimps are laid in their places and the weavers worked across.

Again lay the moss bobbins in their places and work their extra pair through them, without touching the warps.

If the moss bobbins are to be twisted, this is better done before placing the pin across them. The pin is then placed as before, the moss bobbins are laid back, and the weavers worked across.

In working the pair through the moss bobbins, it is well to

pass them through the gimps between each row. Also it must be noted that the tension must be very carefully adjusted when dealing with the moss bobbins, to prevent any part of the work being drawn out of place.

13. **Twisted Lines.**—The pattern for this should be closely pricked.

Hang on an even number of pairs of bobbins, not counting the gimps, and allowing several more pairs than would be used for plain linenwork. To be effective, the ground must be well filled.

Take the left-hand weavers, pass the gimp through them and make a stitch with the first pair of warps. Twist the weavers three times and pass them under the next pair of warps. Stitch with the third pair, twist, and pass under the fourth : and so alternately to the end of the row. Pass the gimp over and under the weavers : twist the weavers and make the edge. On the return row, pass the gimp as before, make a stitch with the first pair of warps (which were passed under by the weavers of the last row), twist, and pass under the second pair and so, as before, alternately to the end of the row. Further rows are a repetition of the above.

As a variation use four pairs of edge bobbins, a pair of weavers being placed at either edge. One pair of weavers, say the left, is now worked through the nearer half of the warps, twisted many times, passed under the farther half, and laid down inside the gimp. Repeat with the right-hand weavers and make both edges, first passing each pair of weavers over and under the gimp on its own side. In passing the second pair of weavers under the warps care must be taken that they shall pass above the first pair. Further rows are repetitions of the foregoing.

It makes little difference whether the right- or left-hand weavers are used first, but the same ones should commence every time for a regular appearance.

A further variation of the second method may be made. After the first rows are made and each pair of weavers laid inside its gimp, take a fresh pair of bobbins, hang their thread on a pin, and pass one under and one over a gimp (say the left) and make the edge. Do the same on the right-hand side.

Commencing from the usual side, work the new weavers through half the warps, twist and pass them under the second half as formerly described, and lay them down inside the weavers already lying inside the gimp, on the side to which they have now worked.

Repeat with the second pair of new weavers.

Now take the weavers lying next the gimp on either side and make the edges. Work the weavers across in their usual method and order, laying them down as before inside those used previously which lie next the gimps.

Worked in this way the little twisted lines will meet at the centre at an angle, which though but slight is prettier than a straight line ; and may be used as a veining for leaves.

14. **Ladder Stitch.**—This has five movements to the stitch instead of four as in cloth stitch. As in that stitch it is made by four bobbins. Cross each pair of warps from right to left.

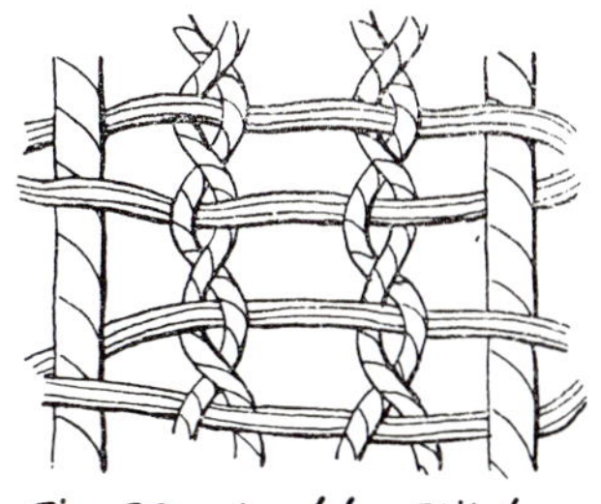

Fig. 52 – Ladder Stitch

1st movement.  With the middle pair lift the left bobbin over the right.

2nd  ,,  With the pair nearest the side *towards* which you are working, lift the right over left.

3rd  ,,  With the middle pair lift the left over right.

4th  ,,  With the pair nearest the side *from* which you work lift the right over left.

5th  ,,  With the middle pair lift the left over right. (See Fig. 52.)

Taking the bobbins as they lie as $A B C D$, the movements are :—

Original position $A B C D$.  Working from $A$ side to $D$ side.

1st movement $A C B D$.
2nd  ,,  $A C D B$.
3rd  ,,  $A D C B$.
4th  ,,  $D A C B$.
5th  ,,  $D C A B$.

As a variation of the above the weavers may be twisted once between every two stitches and at the beginning and end of the row. Do not pull too tightly.

15. **Six Movements.**—This has six movements and is made by four bobbins. The first four movements are as in cloth stitch.

1st left  over right with the middle pair.
2nd right  ,,  left  ,,  ,, right-hand pair.
3rd  ,,  ,,  ,,  ,,  ,, left-  ,,  ,,
4th left  ,,  right  ,,  ,, middle  ,,
5th right  ,,  left  ,,  ,, pair on side *from* which you work.
6th left  ,,  right  ,,  ,, middle pair.  (See Fig. 53.)

Original position *A B C D.*   Working from *A* side to *D* side.
   1st movement *A C B D.*
   2nd    ,,    *A C D B.*
   3rd    ,,    *C A D B.*
   4th    ,,    *C D A B.*
   5th    ,,    *D C A B.*
   6th    ,,    *D A C B.*

This stitch requires to be very carefully pulled up.

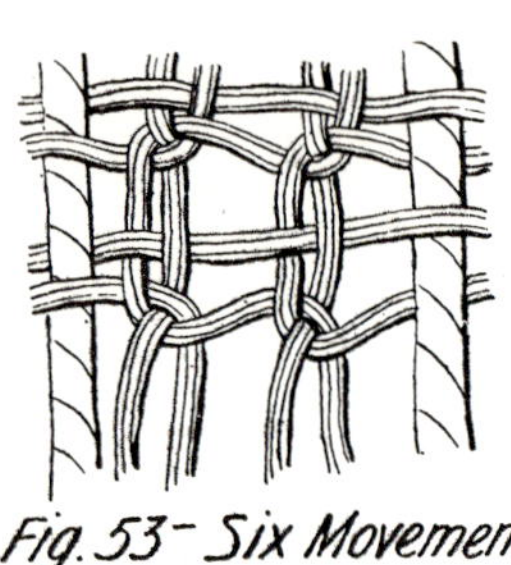

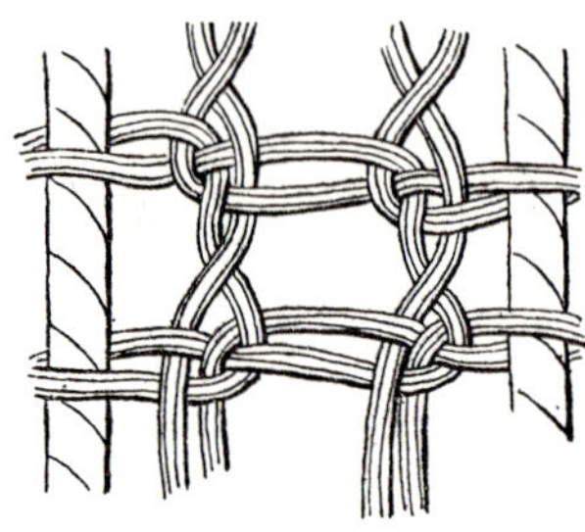

Fig. 53 – Six Movements        Fig. 54 – Seven Movements

16. **Seven Movements.**—This has seven movements and is made with four bobbins.

1st with the pair on the side *towards* which you work lift the right bobbin over the left.

2nd with the middle pair lift the left bobbin over the right.

3rd  ,,  ,,  pair on the side *from* which you work lift the right bobbin over the left.

4th  ,,  ,,  middle pair lift the left bobbin over the right.

5th  ,,  ,,  pair on the side *towards* which you work lift the right bobbin over the left.

6th  ,,  ,,  pair on the side *from* which you work lift the right bobbin over the left.

7th  ,,  ,,  middle pair lift the left bobbin over the right. (See Fig. 54.)

Original position *A B C D.*   Working from *A* side to *D* side.
   1st movement *A B D C.*
   2nd    ,,    *A D B C.*
   3rd    ,,    *D A B C.*
   4th    ,,    *D B A C.*
   5th    ,,    *D B C A.*
   6th    ,,    *B D C A.*
   7th    ,,    *B C D A.*

CHAPTER VIII

# HANGING ON AND FASTENING OFF

### FOR

# BARS, NETS AND FILLINGS

IN working a grounding, either of bars or net, as well as in making a filling for flower centres or other small spaces, great pains must be taken that the hanging on and fastening off be, as far as possible, invisible ; also strong, and well placed for the regular and correct shaping of the work.

Hanging on is not difficult. If hung in separate pairs the bobbin threads should be sewn into edge loops (p. 30) and if fine tied once to prevent slipping. If hung in fours, the thread from one pair is drawn through an edge loop, one bobbin of a second pair drawn through the new loop thus made and one bobbin from each pair tied together. Or instead of the tie, a half- or whole-stitch may be made between the two pairs, which are then separated by a pin set close to the sewing.

In fastening off, it is difficult to prevent the cut ends from working into sight. Each pair is separately sewn into the edge, and may then be twisted and sewn into the upper, or wrong, side of the clothwork, tied and cut off.

In arranging bars, if possible let them finish in a corner, or other place, where they may be tied and cut off without attracting notice.

Before commencing a new row, the student should notice the shape of the space she is filling, both on the right and left. If it be widening, one or more pairs must be hung on. If it narrows, the pair nearest that side must be sewn, tied, and put aside till the space again widens, or be cut off.

If, however, the sides of the space keep at a fairly even distance, the pair nearest either side may be sewn into it, at the level of the second row of unused pinholes and left for use when that row is worked.

To give clearness and simplicity, the directions for nets and fillings will assume that the space to be filled is square.

After a pair has been laid aside it should be twisted both for neatness and to avoid its being clipped off accidentally, when at the end of the work the loose threads are trimmed away.  If the twisted thread has to be brought only a short distance, it may be sewn into the edge at once ; for a longer interval, it is less observed if sewn here and there along a piece of clothwork.

CHAPTER IX

# BARS

THE bar, or " bride," as it is called on the Continent, is the
simplest and quickest method of grounding.   It is important
that enough bars be used to fix every part of the lace into position : especial care being taken with curves and points, which
are liable to be drawn out of shape if tension be unequal.

The bar should be thinner than any part of the pattern ;  or
there may be confusion between the ornament and the ground-
work, and the design may not stand out well.

There is a growing custom among modern workers to form
square or octagonal nets with the bars ;  this for heavy laces has
a good effect, but must be used with discretion for fine work.   In
any case it requires rather a heavy pattern to balance it.

1. **Twists.** — The easiest bar, and that most quickly made, is
formed by sewing a pair of bobbins into an edge, twisting them,
and sewing them into some opposite edge, from whence they may
be again twisted, and carried across another space.   (See Fig. 55.)

To hang on an extra branch, twist the threads in use to the
place where the branch is to hang.   Then thread one of the new
pair of bobbins under the nearest thread of the pair in use and
then over and under its further thread, then draw up both pairs
till the new branch is in place, when both pairs may be twisted
and the work continued.

This bar should only be used for small spaces or common lace.
It is weak in appearance and in strength.

2. **Braids.**—In   some   common   Brussels   and   Bruges   lace
twelve bobbins are attached to an edge, divided in three sets,
braided and used as a bar.   (See Fig. 56.)

Though stronger than No. 1, this bar is also unsuited for good
work.

3A. **Plaits : Plain.**—This is the simplest bar which can be recommended for strength and appearance.   If used over wide
spaces branches must be thrown out at short intervals : or a
regular net formed, which is known as Valenciennes.

The plaited bar is made with four bobbins in repeated half-

stitches.  The movements are three (see p. 59), and they are
continually repeated until the bar is complete.   (See Fig. 57.)
   When a branch is desired, take a fresh pair of bobbins and hang
them on the thread nearest the side on which the bar is wanted.
Set a pin close to the bar, with the four bar bobbins on one side,
and the pair just added on the other.   Make a stitch with the
bar bobbins.   Hang another new pair on the thread of the bar
bobbin next the pin, passing it behind the pin and placing it on
the bar side of the first new pair.   Continue the bar until finished ;

Fig. 55 - Twisted Bar with Branch

and then make the branch in the same manner, with the two fresh
pairs.
   A stronger way of adding the bobbins for a branch is to hang a
pair of bobbins over a pin at the place where the bar is arranged.
Take the nearest bobbin of the bar and put it on the further side
of the pin.   Make a stitch with the bar bobbins, using the nearest
new bobbin in the place of the one put outside the pin and crossing
the first over its neighbour.
   Hang another pair of bobbins over a second pin set close to the
first.   Put the nearest bar bobbin on the further side of the second
pin and continue the bar, using the nearest of the bobbins last
added in place of the one put back.
   The advantage of this method is that the thread of each of the
four bobbins of the branch is continued into the body of the

original bar ; two into the part before the branch and two into that after it.

Care should be taken in pulling up the bobbins for several stitches after adding a new pair.

3B. **Plaits with Single Thread Loops.**—The bar is made as above, but at short intervals a pin is inserted close to the last stitch made, and the thread of the nearest bobbin passed round it from the outside, pulled up and the bar continued.   (See Fig. 58.)

3C. **Plaits with Picots.**—This is like No. 3A, but with picots (p. 44) added on one side at short intervals.

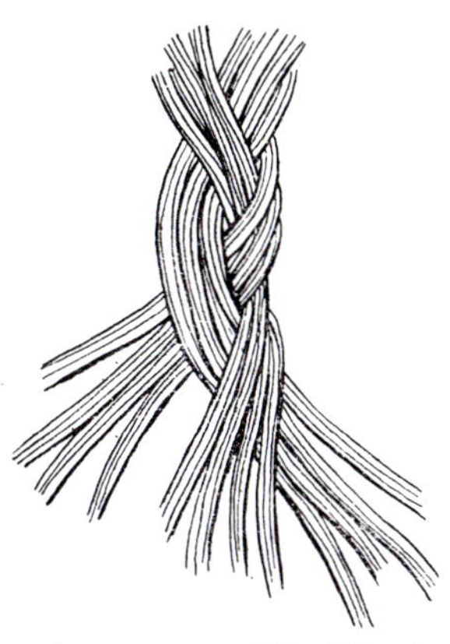

Fig. 56 - Braided Bar

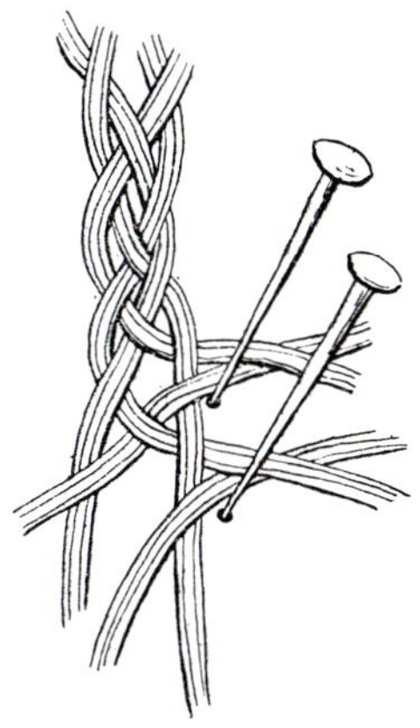

Fig. 57 - Plaited Bar Plain

4A. **Guimpe Ten Stick or Ordinary.**—On one side this bar has the regular cord and loop edge.   On the other, it is finished by stem or turning stitch.   This is a half-stitch followed by a linen stitch, worked by the same four bobbins.   (See Fig. 59.)

The name " ten stick " is given, because it is most frequently made by five pairs of bobbins, though for light work only four may be used.   It is frequently made for stems of flowers (hence the name " stem stitch ") ; for this six or more pairs may be required.

4B. **Pearl Pin, or Picot.**—This is made in the same way as No. 4A, but with picots (p. 44) instead of the cord and loop edge.

4C. **Double Stem Stitch.**—This is a bar with stem stitch at each edge : its difficulty lies in having no pinholes by which it can be fixed in place ; but small bridges of paper may be laid across it and closely pinned down for that purpose.   (See Fig. 60.)   If pins be used at centre or edge they are apt to leave marks.

4D. **Plaited Loops.**—The plaited loop may be added to any bar which is worked with eight or more bobbins, but has a heavy

Fig. 58 - Plaited Bar with Single Thread Loops

appearance and is not often used for fine laces.  In making it, a pin is placed close to the bar and a plait of repeated half-stitches, sufficient to go round the pin, made by the four nearest bobbins. The plait is then passed out below the pin and brought round it

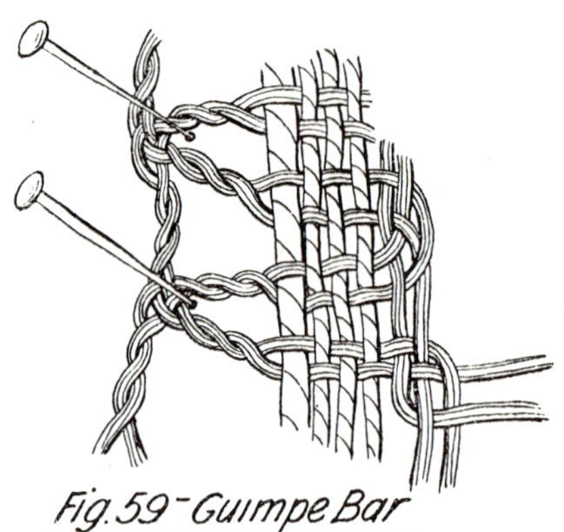

Fig. 59 - Guimpe Bar

from above to the bar again ; where the bobbins are laid in right order beside the others.  (See Fig. 61.)

5A. **Linen Stitch Cord.**—The writer has not found this cord any-where in  her researches in English and  foreign museums, and believes it to be new.  It is strong, of light appearance, and well made, is suitable for the finest work.  Care should be taken to pull up the bobbins with a firm, even tension.  Directions for working are given on p. 57.

5B. **Linen Stitch Cord : Lined.**—This is a thicker variation of No. 5A. Directions are given on p. 57.

The weavers must go evenly round and round. Every circle

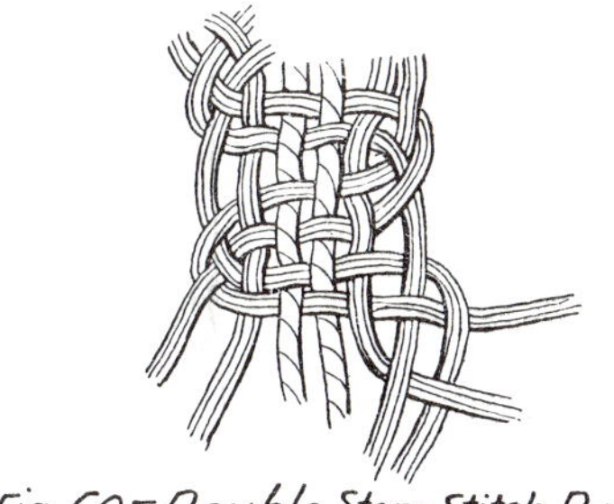

Fig. 60 – Double Stem Stitch Bar

should be pushed up close to the last by raising the warps in pairs, while the weavers are gently pulled. The weavers must not be crossed or the smoothness of the work would be spoiled.

6. **Open Work.**—The pricking for this bar consists of two rows of pinholes about ten to the inch and those in each row alternate

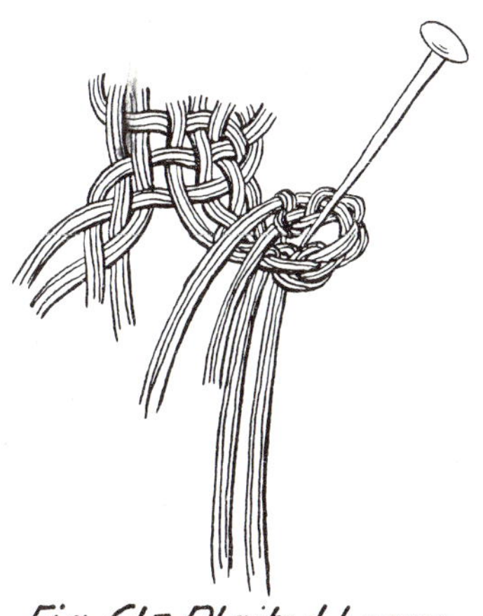

Fig. 61 – Plaited Loops

with each other, each hole being at the same distance from the holes in the other row as from those in its own.

Half-stitches may be used, but linen stitches make a stronger bar that keeps in better shape.

Three pairs of bobbins are hung on, and a stitch made by the

two pairs on the side of the highest pinhole.   Each pair is twisted
and a pin set in the highest hole between the two pairs just
worked.   The third pair is now twisted and a stitch made between

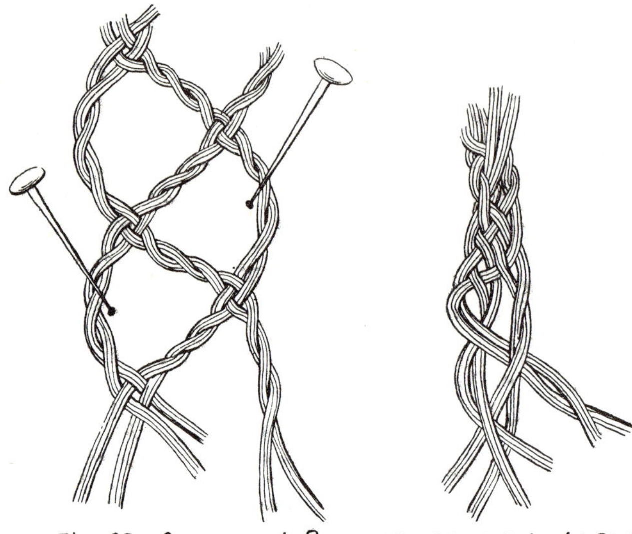

Fig. 62 - Open-work Bar     Fig. 63 - Stitched & Plaited Bar

it and the middle pair.   Twist each pair three or more times,
set a pin in the next lower hole between the pair just stitched.
Repeat till the bar is finished, working an outside with a middle
pair each time a pinhole is used.   (See Fig. 62.)

The pattern will have quite a different appearance if two pairs
of bobbins are left outside the pin each time one is set.

7. **Stitch and Plait.**—Hang on three pairs of bobbins and twist
each pair twice.

         Pass the left pair over the middle pair.
         ,,     ,, right ,,    ,,    ,,    ,,    ,,
         ,,     ,, left  ,,    ,,    ,,    ,,    ,,

Pull up each pair carefully.

With the right-hand pair work cloth stitch through the two
others, and pull up again very thoroughly.   Twist each pair
twice, and repeat every movement in turn.   (See Fig. 63.)

This bar is strong, rich-looking and quickly made, but needs to
be carefully and frequently pulled up.

CHAPTER X

# NETS: PLAIN

I. **LILLE.**—With the exception of Torchon (which is scarcely worthy of the name) this is the simplest of nets, and from it, in various ways, all other nets may be developed. It is very popular both in England and Belgium, forming the main grounding of old and modern Midland "Point", and having been largely used for Continental "Cap Laces." Lille is quick and easy to make and adapt to different shapes and corners, and is quite strong.

To prepare a new pattern for it correctly, a square-ruled paper should be firmly pinned over the material on which the pattern is to be pricked. If the ruling be about twenty squares to the linear inch, a pinhole may be made in each alternate square for the first row. Leave the next row of squares untouched, and in the third prick each alternate square, placing each pinhole under the square that separates the pinholes of the first row. Leave a row of squares unused between each two rows of pinholes, and let the holes in each row be under the spaces in the one above. When this is used as a grounding in Honiton, Duchesse, etc., each pair of bobbins should be sewn into a loop in the upper part of the space to be filled.

The principle of this and of most bobbin nets is that stitches are made separately, each by a group of bobbins, which groups are placed at intervals in a row. In the next row the groups are divided; a new group is formed by half the bobbins from the left- and half from the right-hand neighbour. This repeated in succeeding rows shows strands of thread running from group to group. It is these strands that form the net. For neatness, strength and beauty, the strands are always twisted.

Nets of this class may be made diagonally from right to left; beginning with the left-hand top corner: or worked in lines straight across the space to be filled. The latter method being easier for a student to learn is used here. Once the method is understood the student can work either way.

Hang the bobbins in pairs (the number of pairs should be even) at equal distances along the upper border of the space to be filled, twisting each pair three times.

Make a half-stitch between the two pairs on the left; twist each pair twice, and set a pin between the pairs in the nearest hole, which should be half-way between the two pairs and at a distance below them of one pinhole from another.  Repeat with each group of two pairs along the row.   (See Fig. 64.)

If the space be square, one pair of bobbins at each end of the row is sewn into the side at the level of the pinholes of the second row and left for use in the third row.

For the second row, take a pair from each neighbouring set, make a half-stitch and set a pin as before.

The pairs may be twisted after making a stitch, or before the next one, as preferred, but it must be remembered that the half-stitch leaves one twist, so that only two more will be needed.

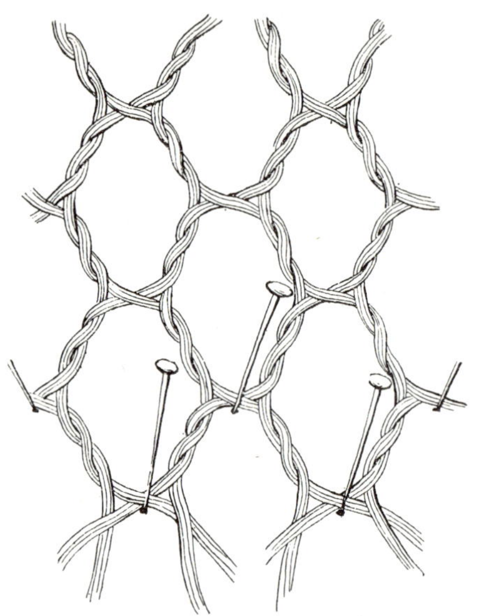

Fig. 64.- Lille

The third row will begin with a pair sewn to the side, marking the fact that the same sets are used as in the first row.  The working will be repeated.

2. **Spotted Net : Point d'Esprit.**—This is made on the Lille pattern, with a mark added where each spot is required.

The net is made like No. 1, with at every mark a square leaf (p. 101) worked instead of the usual half-stitch.  No pin is used for the leaf and only one twist is given to each pair before and after it.

3. **Chantilly.**—The working is the same as for Lille (No. 1), but two pins instead of one are set to divide the pairs after each stitch.   (See Fig. 65.)

For the pattern, make two holes in neighbouring squares, miss two squares and repeat. Miss two rows of squares between each two rows of pinholes, and make the pinholes in each row under the squares that were missed in the row above them.

The pattern should be pricked on closely ruled paper, and is best made with very fine thread. The mesh looks rounder than the Lille.

4. **Torchon.**—This is worked on the same pattern as the Lille (No. 1) and makes a close ground.

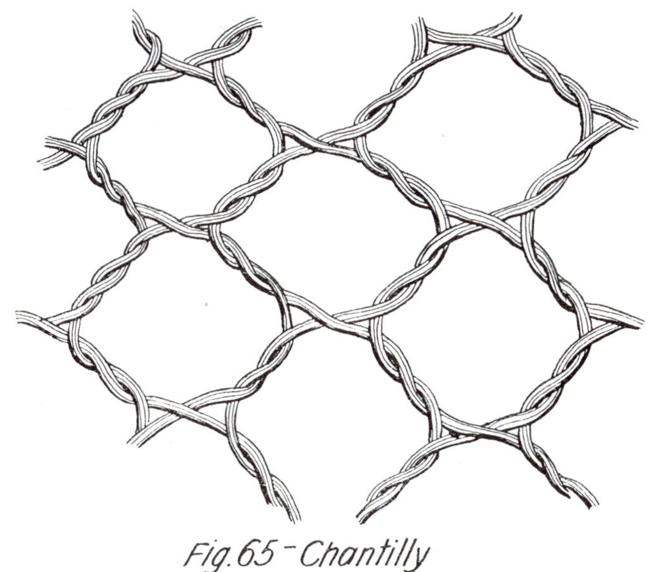

Fig. 65 - Chantilly

Use an even number of pairs of bobbins, and hang each pair separately along the upper border of the space, rather near together, crossing each pair once. Make a half-stitch with the two pairs on the left, set a pin between them, and enclose it by another half-stitch. Repeat with each two pairs in succession along the row.

In the second row, as usual with nets, the first and last pair of bobbins will be sewn into the side twice, and left ready for the third row. The rest of the stitches will be made with one pair from each of neighbouring sets. This is done throughout the row, and further rows are worked in the same way. (See Fig. 66.)

The net has a heavy appearance, but, if the pinholes are further apart and an extra two twists given to each pair after each two half-stitches it is lighter.   Or a second twist to the bobbins before enclosing the pin is perhaps an improvement.   But these latter ways are not strictly Torchon.

5. **Dieppe.**—This is worked in the same way as Torchon (No. 4), but with two twists after each two half-stitches instead of one.

6. **Brussels.**—The present net is very strong and beautiful. It is made on the Lille pattern (No. 1) and in the same way, except that, after placing the pin, two half-stitches are made to enclose

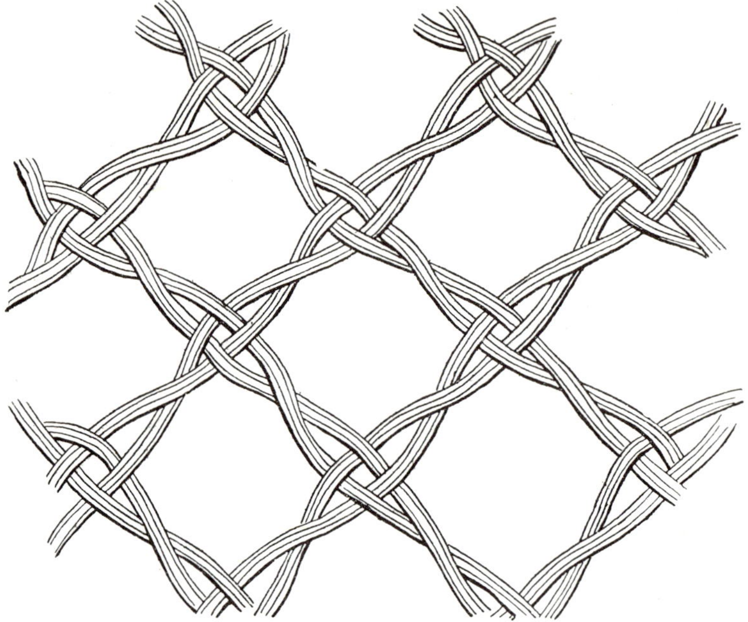

Fig. 66 - Torchon

it, or, technically, cover it.   The half-stitch is known in Belgium as a " demi-passée," and two " demi-passées " following each other are called a " passée double."   (See Fig. 67.)

7. **Mechlin.**—This net has even a greater reputation than the Brussels, being made generally with exceedingly fine thread.   It differs from Brussels (No. 6) only in the number of stitches when placing the pin.   Two half-stitches are made (a " passée double "), the pin is set, and is covered by two more half-stitches.

**Bar Nets.**—Most nets made with twisted bobbins may be worked by using a bar of four or more threads instead of the twisted cord, giving thus the same general appearance but a bolder effect.

Valenciennes in this manner is developed from Lille. The varieties obtained in this way are specially useful in dealing with centres of flowers, and also for contrasted groundings.

8. **Valenciennes.**—In the Lille net (p. 84) practically the whole mesh was twisted. In Brussels and Mechlin two portions of it are formed by plaits. But in Valenciennes the whole mesh, the whole lace, in fact, is formed by plaiting. The net is mostly

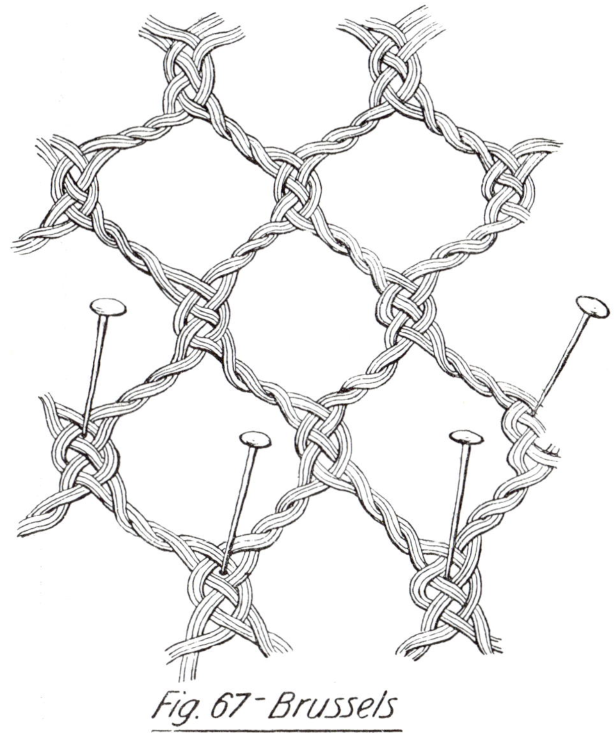

Fig. 67 - Brussels

used for narrow border laces, but makes an excellent ground, or filling, for any fine lace.

The valuable old " false Valenciennes " is of a different character and has its grounding of " Boule-de-Neige " or " Snowball " net (p. 98).

Valenciennes proper is made in two ways, according to the shape of mesh desired.

8A. **Round or Hexagonal Valenciennes.**—If a pricked pattern be used, it will be the same as for Lille (p. 84). In Belgium it is generally worked without pins, except in a border lace, for the head, foot and ornaments (flowers, spots, etc.). That is to say, no pins are used for the actual net.

Hang on the bobbins in sets of eight. Take the first set, to the left, cross each pair and make a half-stitch with the two middle pairs and work four even half-stitches (two passées doubles) with the left four bobbins, then sew them to the side level with the pinholes.

Do the same with the last set on the right, working them four times, and sewing to the side level with the first row of pinholes.

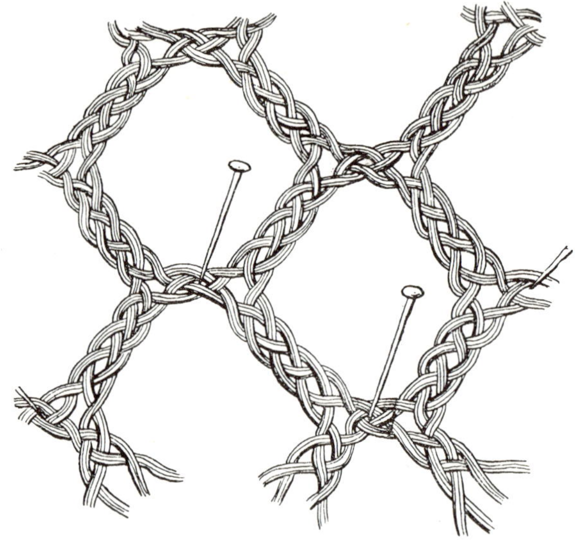

Fig. 68 – Valenciennes, Round Mesh

Half-stitch the middle pairs of each set and work four stitches with its right-hand four and its left-hand four.

The working so far is the same for both round and square meshes. To unite these bars, make a half-stitch with the two middle pairs of the first two sets of four on the left that are not already sewn, that is with the pair in each set that is nearest to the other. Set a pin between them in the nearest hole, and close the pin with another half-stitch. (See Fig. 68.)

Repeat with each two sets along the row.

The next row will be the same as the first, except that the bobbins will be already half-stitched and crossed, from the half-stitches, and that when the bars are united they take their companion bar from their opposite side, the ones that stitched with a right-hand bar taking a left, and *vice versa.*

In the second row the bars which were sewn to the side in the first row will be worked and stitched with the bars respectively on their right and left.

The working for each row is mainly the same, differing only in whether the side bars are used or sewn and if those in the middle pair with their right or left neighbours.

Fig. 69 - Valenciennes, Square Mesh

8B. **Square Valenciennes.**—For this, the bobbins are hung and the bars made as for the round, and the first stitch to connect each two bars is made, as before, by taking one pair from each bar, making a half-stitch and setting a pin between them. The second stitch, however, is quite different. It is made by taking the two unused pairs from the two bars and making a half-stitch with them. The pin may be withdrawn and reset between the last used pairs, or preferably left in place, enclosed by the last stitch. (See Fig. 69.)

It is quite impossible to make this type of lace as flat as the round, for, from the method of working, the threads must cross. It is strong and much used in Belgium for narrow laces. Many, however, think the smooth and even finish of the round mesh to leave little to be desired.

The town of Valenciennes has long ceased to produce lace for commercial purposes, the shops there obtaining their supplies from Belgium.

**Fancy Nets.**—With the exception of Chantilly, our preceding nets may be worked upon like patterns; differing only in the closeness of their pinholes. In working, they differ also but little.

In the present group, the meshes, though made in a manner derived from Lille (p. 84), are differently placed, and so need other arrangements of the pinholes. If the student can obtain for study a piece of any net which she wishes to make, or even a clear picture of it, and will also consider the pricked pattern, she will find it of great assistance to a clear understanding of methods and effects.

9. **Maiden's Net (Point de la Vierge).**—In preparing the pattern for this, on squared paper of twenty-six squares to the inch, leave three unused squares between every two pinholes, and one row of squares unused between every two rows of pinholes.

Place the pinholes of the second row under the middle square of the unused ones, which divide the pinholes.

The pinholes of the third row are set directly under those of the first; and those of the fourth row are placed under the pinholes of the second, etc.

In preparing this pattern, connect the pinholes by pen or pencil marks, forming small diamonds.

Connect the second pinhole in the first row with the two nearest ones in the second row and those with the one midway between them in the third.

From each alternate pinhole of the first row start a diamond, finishing it, as above, with two beneath it in the second, and one in the third row.

For the working, hang two pairs of bobbins on the left, above the upper pinhole of the first diamond, and two pairs on the right. Of these four pairs take the two middle ones. Cross each pair and make a half-stitch. Set a pin between the two pairs in the upper pinhole of the diamond; and enclose the pin with another half-stitch.

Take the pair on the extreme left, and, crossing the bobbins, make a half-stitch with the pair next on the right. Set a pin between the pairs in the left-hand pinhole of the diamond, and enclose with a half-stitch.

Cross the outside right-hand pair, and stitch with the pair next on the left. Set a pin between the pairs in the right-hand pin-hole of the diamond and enclose it with a half-stitch.

For the last pinhole, take the two middle pairs and make a

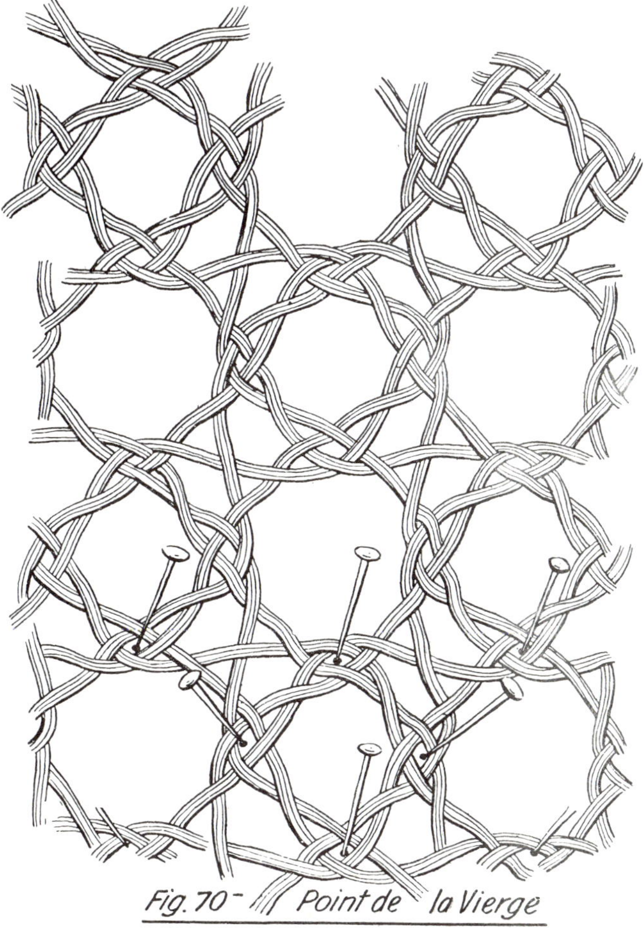



half-stitch; set a pin between them in the lowest hole of the diamond and enclose it with a half-stitch. Work a half-stitch with the two left-hand and another with the two right-hand pairs and the first diamond is complete. (See Fig. 70.)

Every diamond in the first row is worked in the same manner, only sufficient bobbins for the diamond in hand being hung on at one time, for unworked bobbins give much unnecessary trouble.

For the second row, take the two pairs of bobbins on the right, and the two pairs on the left nearest the upper hole of each

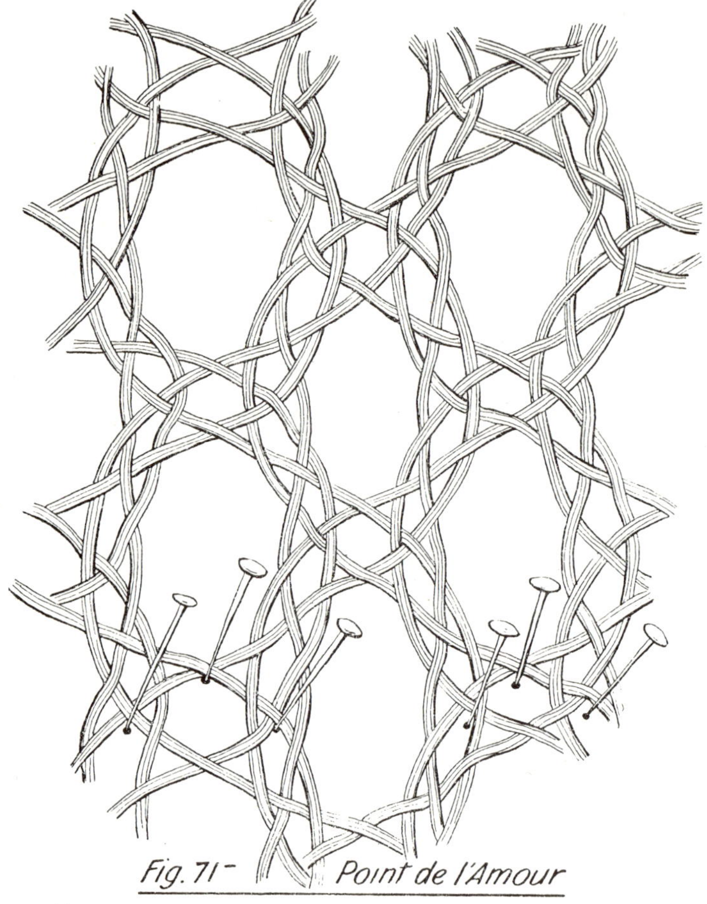

Fig. 71.      Point de l'Amour

new diamond for a fresh set, and work them in the same way as for the first diamond.

10. **Cupid's Net (Point de l'Amour).**—This is worked on the same pattern as "Point de la Vierge," and there is great similarity in the working. It is a lighter ground than the last and forms a link between it and "Point de Mariage."

Follow the directions in No. 9 (p. 90) for placing the four pins of the diamond, but omit the half-stitch after each pin has been set. (See Fig. 71.)

After the fourth pin is in place make a half-stitch both with the two right-hand and left-hand pairs to complete the diamond.

11. **Wedding Net (Point de Mariage).** — The paper for this pattern should be very finely ruled, at least thirty squares to the inch. Like that for No. 9, this pattern is pricked in diamonds, only it has eight holes to each diamond and four of those belong also to four neighbouring diamonds.

The first row has seven squares unused between the adjacent pinholes, and a row of squares is left untouched between every two rows of pinholes.

In the second row three squares are left between every two pinholes, which are placed right and left of those squares that are under the pinholes of the first row.

The first pinhole of the third row is placed in the square halfway between the pinholes of the first row and seven squares are left between the pinholes.

The fourth row is like the second, each pinhole being directly under one of that row.

The fifth row completes the first diamond, and is the first row of the second. It is like the first row, and every pinhole is under one of that row. The rows for the completion of the second diamond will correspond to the like rows in the first.

For the working round the upper pinhole of the first diamond, two pairs of bobbins should be hung to the left, and two to the right, just above the nearest pinholes of the second row. Make a half-stitch with the two left pairs and another with the two right ones, giving each pair an extra twist.

Make a half-stitch with the two middle pairs and set a pin in the upper pinhole of the diamond between them. Twist each pair again, make another half-stitch and again twist each pair.

Make a half-stitch with the two left-hand pairs and set a pin between them in the left upper pinhole of the diamond. Twist each pair again, make another half-stitch, and again twist each pair. Repeat with the two right pairs and the right-hand pinhole.

Hang a pair on the left edge just above the extreme left pinhole of the diamond, twist twice, make a stitch with the next pair, and twist again. Set a pin between the pairs in the extreme left pinhole of the diamond, make another half-stitch, and twist again. Lay down the left-hand pair (ready to be sewn into the edge and used for the next diamond) and make a half-stitch with the next pair on the right. Set a pin in the lowest left-hand hole, twist and cover the pin with another half-stitch.

Hang four pairs for the next diamond and work them in the same way as for the first, until the first three pins have been set and covered.

Take the right-hand pair from the first diamond, and the left-hand pair from the second, and make a half-stitch. Set a pin between the pairs, in the hole which connects the two diamonds, twist both pairs, make another half-stitch, and twist again.

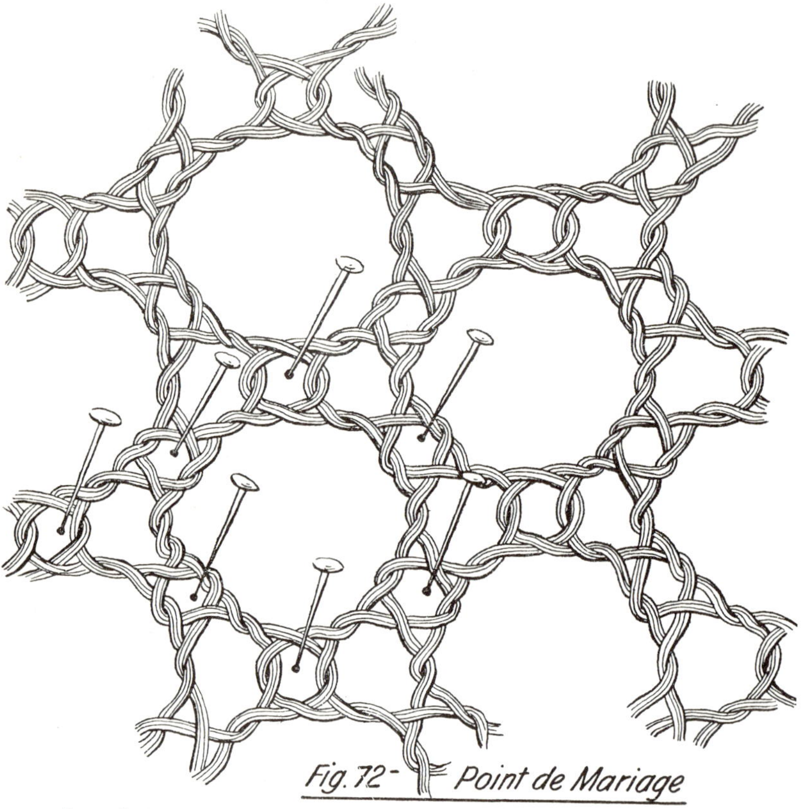

Fig. 72 - Point de Mariage

Lay down the right-hand pair, take the pair next on the left, make a half-stitch, and set a pin between the pairs in the lowest right-hand hole of the first diamond. Twist each pair, make a half-stitch, twist again, and lay down the right-hand pair. Take the pair next on the left, make a half-stitch, set a pin between the pairs in the lowest hole of the diamond, twist both pairs, make another half-stitch, and twist each pair again.

This completes the first diamond, and is also the upper hole of the next below it. (See Fig. 72.)

The other diamonds are worked in the same way, bobbins being hung on or thrown off at the edge as required. In any case, the net must be fastened to the side at every row.

12. **Friendship Net (Point de l'Amitié).**—This, though not quite so attractive in appearance as No. 11, is perhaps stronger.

The directions may be taken from No. 11 (p. 93), except that after any half-stitch made before the setting of a pin, no extra twist is given with either pair. Also when the half-stitch after the pin has been made, the bobbins are firmly pulled up before they have their second twist.

13. **Ring Net.**—In preparing the pattern for this, as for the preceding nets, one row of squares must be left unused between every two rows of pinholes. The first row is pricked with three unused squares between every two pinholes.

In the second row the pinholes are midway between those of the first row.

In the third row the distance between the pinholes is the same, but each pinhole is placed under one in the row above.

As will be noted, two rows have the pinholes one beneath the other, changing the position of the pinholes at every third row to a place midway between those of the rows above.

For working, hang two pairs of bobbins right and left above each of the three first pinholes on the left of the first row. Make a half-stitch, with the first and second pairs, and set a pin between them in the first hole, twist each pair, make another half-stitch, and twist again. Repeat with the other sets.

Sew to the side with the left-hand pair, twist twice and leave them. Take the pair next on the right, and the left-hand pair of the second set, make a half-stitch, and set a pin between them in the nearest hole of the second row. Twist both pairs, make another half-stitch, set a pin between them in the pinhole just below in the third row, and twist both pairs again.

Take the right-hand pair of the second set and the left pair of the third, make a half-stitch, set a pin between the pairs in the nearest hole of the second row, twist, make another half-stitch, and set a pin between the pairs in the hole just below in the third row. More bobbins are now hung and worked as before to the end of the row. This is a variety of Torchon. (See Fig. 73.)

The next and succeeding rows are worked in the same way; the new set being always formed by one pair from the left and one from the right.

Sewings should be made once at the level of the upper and once of the lower holes.

14. **French Net (Point de Paris).**—The pattern for this ground

is the same as for Lille (p. 84).   This net is developed from Lille by two additions :—

First, every time a pin is placed it is enclosed by a second half-stitch.

Next, after each row of pins has been set and enclosed, an extra pair of bobbins is hung at one edge, worked through to the other, and sewn there.   This straight thread running through gives the characteristic style of the lace.

For working, two pairs of bobbins are hung above the first pin-hole on the left.   A half-stitch is made, a pin set between the

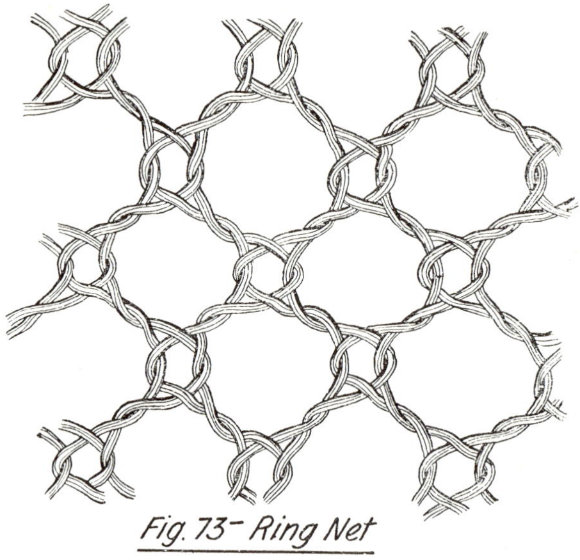

Fig. 73- Ring Net

pairs, and enclosed by another half-stitch.   This is repeated for each pinhole in the row.

A pair of bobbins is then sewn on the edge at one side, just below the level of the pins, crossed once and a whole stitch made with it and the nearest pair.   Another twist is made with both pairs, and another cloth stitch made with the weavers and the next pair.   This is repeated to the end of the row : always a twist and a stitch.   Care must be taken that the bobbins hung from above keep their twists.   When the last pair has been worked the travelling bobbins are crossed and sewn to the edge, twisted three times, and sewn again just below the level of the next pin-holes and left.

The next row will be the same as the first except that each

stitch will be made with one pair of bobbins from the right and one from the left-hand set.

The fourth row is made like the second, by the travelling bobbins. And further rows are alternately like the first and the second. Note that the sets are changed with each row in which pins are placed. (See Fig. 74.)

A light and pretty variation of this is made by placing the pinholes wider apart and giving an extra twist in each case where the threads are crossed.

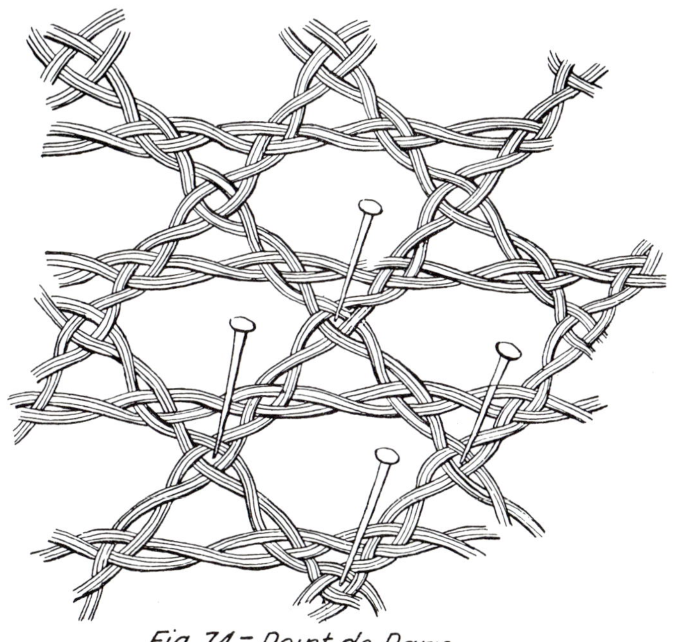

Fig. 74 – Point de Paris

15. **Striped Net.**—For this pattern three squares are left between every two pinholes and three rows of squares between every two rows of pinholes, if ruled paper is used of twenty-six or thirty squares to the inch.

The pinholes in each row are placed under those of the last.

The ground is worked in the same way as " Paris " (p. 95), except that the sets are not changed. The pinholes being one below the other, the same four bobbins are always used for the same line of pinholes. The only other change for this net is that the travelling bobbins should have three twists between each two sets of four and two between every two pairs.

16. **Waved Stripe.**—This is worked on the same pattern as the
" Ring," and made alternately like the " Paris " (p. 95) and
" Striped " (p. 97) grounds.

When about to set a pin, if its hole be below that of the last
row, the same set of bobbins will be used for it.

If the hole be between those of the last row, one pair must be
taken from the left and one from the right set.

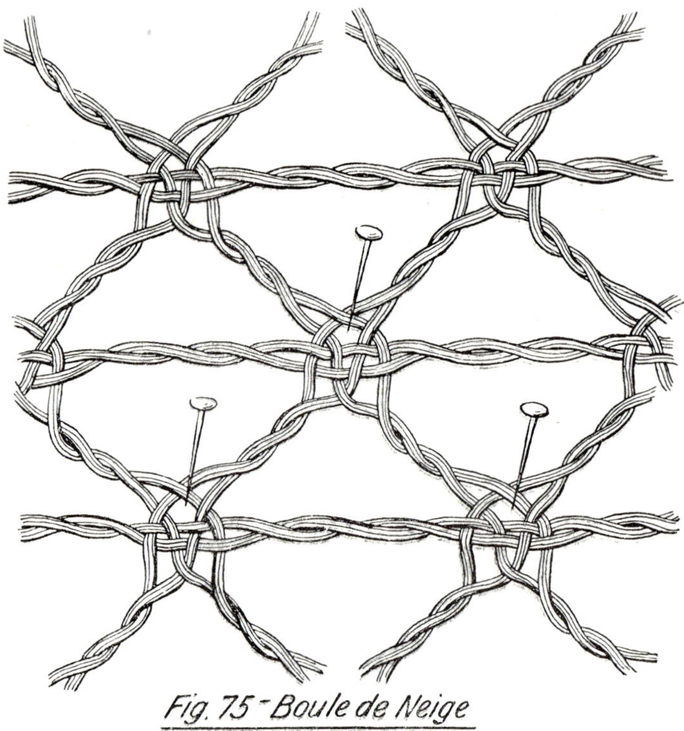

Fig. 75 - Boule de Neige

This ground is better worked with a very fine thread and
closely pricked pattern, and the travelling pair should have three
twists between the sets and two between the pairs.

17. **Cobweb (Boule-de-Neige).**—This is a very old ground and
characteristic of the so-called " fausse Valenciennes," a most
valuable lace.

The pattern is the same as for Lille, but should not be very
closely pricked unless the thread is extremely fine.

To fill a space with this net, the highest row of pinholes should
lie under the upper edge as a guide, two pairs of bobbins being

hung at each pinhole, except at the two ends, where only one pair is hung.

Beginning from the left, the single pair is taken with the left pair of the next set and each is twisted three times. Make a half-stitch or whole if preferred and set a pin between the pairs in the hole that lies just below and between them. Repeat along the row, taking one pair from each adjacent set. Hang a pair at one side level with the pinholes, twist three times, and work through the first set in whole stitch, which must be carefully pulled up and adjusted, the pin being taken out and replaced till the end of the row. The travellers are then twisted three times and worked through the next set ; this being repeated to the end of the row, when the travellers are twisted, sewn into the edge, again twisted, and sewn again level with the next row of pinholes and left.

The pins are now withdrawn, a half-stitch or whole, if that is used, is made with each set along the row, and each pair carefully pulled up and twisted twice (making, with the half-stitch cross, three twists in all). The twists may be made now, or when picking up the bobbins to make the next stitch. (See Fig. 75.)

The illustration is of a ground worked in half-stitch except when the travelling bobbins are used.

The next row is worked like the first by taking one pair from each set. The single pairs, at the ends, are twisted as the others and kept close against the sides with a pin ; the travelling bobbins work through them, but do not twist afterwards, sewing into the side at once.

The ground is worked entirely in this way and should look like minute cobwebs.

# CHAPTER XI

# FILLINGS

**LEAF STITCH.**—The English " filling " (or Belgian " a jours ") is used for small enclosed spaces, such as the centres of flowers, medallions, etc., which form a prominent part of the design and from their small size can be afforded a richer treatment. The filling most in use both in old and modern lace of the Brussels and Honiton type, as well as in Maltese, is known by many names, that of leaf stitch being among the most descriptive of them. Leaf stitch is made by three straight threads held together by a fourth thread woven in and out between and around them.

English Midland workers use the following method of forming the leaves :—

Having sewn two pairs of bobbins at a short distance one from the other, and twisted each pair, three bobbins are laid on the pillow and the fourth held in the hand and worked in and out, backwards and forwards between them.

The right-hand bobbin is taken as the weaver and passed under the middle bobbin from the right over the left-hand bobbin, and then under it from the left over the middle bobbin and under the right-hand bobbin from the left. These movements complete one stitch, which must next be pulled up by gently pulling the weaving thread and regulating the position of the three others, which form, as it were, the framework. These must be opened more widely if the leaf is to widen and put nearer together if it is to be narrowed ; while, naturally, they are kept in the same position as long as the leaf continues to be made of the same width.

There are other methods of making this stitch. The following way was taught to the writer, in the seventies, by a lace worker, who had been instructed in the old Devon lace schools from the age of four years ; probably starting before 1845.

In this Devon way one pair of bobbins is held in each hand : the bobbin used for weaving being worked in and out, backwards and forwards between them as in the Midland method, while the warps are also regulated for position and tension.

Another style of working, the Belgian, is probably the best, but requires exactness in the position of the hands. The left bobbin is held by the thumb against the forefinger of the left hand, between its upper and second joints. The middle bobbin is held by the same thumb against the tip of the forefinger; while the third is held by the tip of the second finger against the ball of the thumb. The free end of each bobbin should rest in the palm of the hand. One of the right-hand bobbins should be chosen as the weaver.

This stitch is used for very many beautiful fillings; the simplest of which is the single square, used as a centre for a flower, or other small space.

Fig. 76 - Square Leaf

IA. **Single Square.**—Mark by pins, or simply by the eye, four loops, at equal distances from each other, in the edge surrounding the space to be filled.

Hang a pair of bobbins in each of the two upper loops. Twist each pair three times and make four leaf stitches, bringing back the weaver to be one of its original pair and supporting that pair with a pin. (See Fig. 76.)

Twist the left-hand pair three times; sew to the edge at the spot formerly chosen, and tie. Do not cut off until the second pair is also tied unless you are an expert.

Take up the right-hand pair very lightly and carefully, twist three times, sew, tie and cut off both pairs.

IB. **Single Oval.**—Hang on as before. Twist each pair three times, make a cloth stitch and pull up. Make six leaf stitches, the first rather tight if the leaf is to be pointed, but looser if a round end is preferred.   Widen by loosening the weaving thread in the middle stitches and by opening out the warps.

Narrow again and finish with a cloth stitch.   (See Fig. 77.) Support the right-hand pair with a pin, while the left are twisted and secured.   Sew the right-hand pair, tie and cut off both pairs.

1C. **Beehive.**—Begin as for the oval ; but make only four stitches and finish as for the square.   (See Fig. 78.)

1D. **Hour-glass.**—Begin as for the square, but gradually tighten the third and fourth stitches.   Then make a cloth stitch : loosen the two next stitches, work two more, and finish as a square. (See Fig. 79.)

2. **Leaf with Raised Rib.**—The writer believes this to be quite new.   It is stronger than the ordinary leaf stitch and less liable

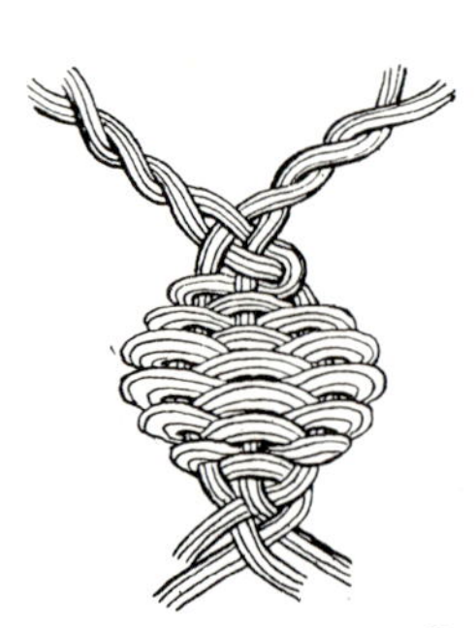

Fig. 77 - Oval Leaf

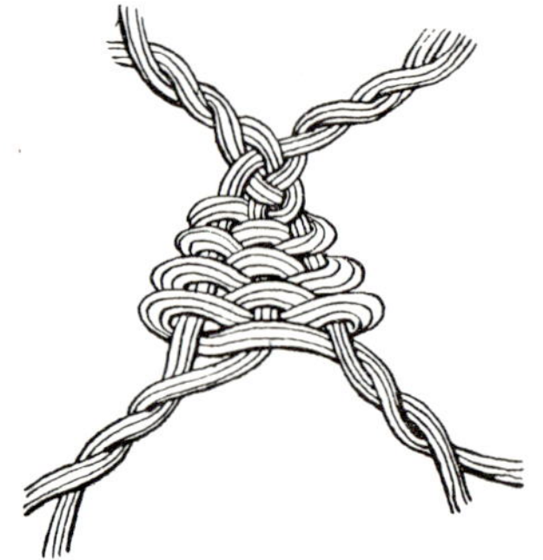

Fig. 78 - Beehive Leaf

to slip out of shape.   The square, oval, beehive and hour-glass shapes can be made in this equally well as in the plain.   Hold three bobbins as in the Belgian method of making leaf stitch (p. 101).   Take the weaver in the right hand, pass it over the middle bobbin and then under it from the left.   Pull up the thread and pass the weaver over the left bobbin and under it from the left, over the middle one and under the right from the left.   This completes the stitch and must be well drawn up.   For each stitch the movements are repeated.   (See Fig. 80.)   A leaf-stitch pin to support each warp will be found useful, if it prove difficult to hold the bobbins in the hand.

3A. **Cross with Open Centre.**—Mark, with pins, four equi-distant places in the border of the space for which this filling is intended and mark also its centre with a pinhole.

Hang two pairs of bobbins right and left of each of the two

upper marks, four pairs in all. Take the left-hand set, and twist each pair three times. Make eight square even leaf stitches (p. 100) and twist each pair again three times. Support the bobbins by a pin set between the pairs on the left of the centre hole.

Work the right-hand set in the same way and set a pin between them on the right of the centre hole.* (See Fig. 81.)

Now consider. The idea is to work one set of bobbins through the other, and in doing it to make an open-work centre by twisting between the stitches.

Take the left-hand set to work through with and begin by working its right-hand pair through the left-hand pair of the right set.

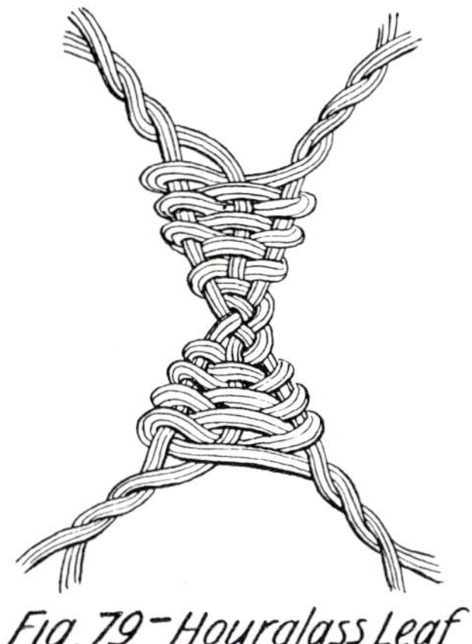

Fig. 79—Hourglass Leaf

Fig. 80—Raised Rib Leaf

Set a pin in the centre hole between the pairs just worked and twist both pairs three times. Work your travelling pair, which will be next the pin on the right-hand side, through the extreme right-hand pair, twist both pairs and lay them down.* Take the pair on the extreme left, work through the next pair, twist each pair three times, and lay down the pair now on the left : work a stitch with the two middle pairs, and twist both three times.

If the work be right, there will be a centre of five meshes of net. Three of these will be enclosed and finished, and the other two ready to enclose by working the other two arms of the cross. These are made, like the two first, by working eight square even leaf stitches. Each pair is then twisted three times and cut off.

3B. **Cross with Crossed Centre.**—This is worked like No. 3A, as far as the second asterisk.

At this stage one pair from the left has been worked through the two right-hand pairs and laid aside. These two right-hand pairs will be twisted. Of these pass the left-hand pair over the right. Work the pair on the extreme left through the pair next to it, twist each pair three times and work the travellers through the next pair on the right; twist each pair three times, and finish as in No. 1A by eight leaf stitches, twisting sewing, and cutting off.

3C. **Cross with Closed Centre.**—Make this like No. 3A to the first asterisk. Then work the left central pair of bobbins through

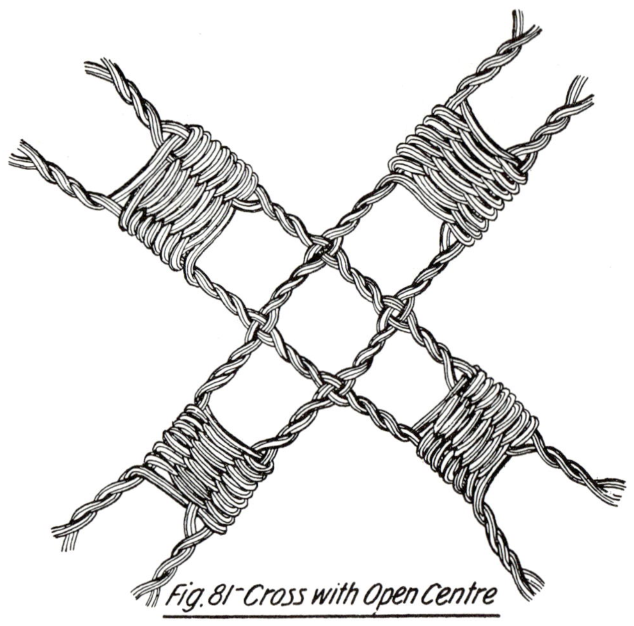



the two pairs on the right; twist them three times and lay them down. Take the outside pair on the left, work through the two pairs next on the right, and twist each pair three times. Finish, as in No. 3A, by eight leaf stitches, sewing, and cutting off.

4. **Chequered Square Leaf.**—A pricked pattern is not absolutely necessary, but is convenient and should be the same as for No. 7 (p. 106).

Hang on the bobbins in sets of four at regular distances, placing single pairs at the two sides.

Take the two pairs nearest to the left, twist each pair three times, make four or more even leaf stitches, and again twist each pair three times. Put in a pin to support the bobbins.

Sew the left-hand pair to the edge, twist again, and again sew at the place where it will be ready for the third row.

Do the same with the two right-hand pairs. Work the other sets in the row in the same way, except sewing.

The second row will be worked as above between the middle sets, using one pair from each right- and left-hand set, not touching either side. In the third row the pairs at the side will be used again, and so on alternately till the space is filled.

If the Beehive, Oval or Hour-glass shape is worked, the pricking to be used will be that for Ring net (No. 13 on p. 95).

An extra pin is set where a whole stitch is made in the middle. If the worker is not an expert it will be found better to prick the pattern on rather a larger scale than is usual for the nets.

Fillings may be varied by making the horizontal rows nearer together than the perpendicular ones or *vice versa*.

5. **Crossed Leaf Chequers.**—The pattern for this is pricked in squares, the first row of pinholes being at the same distance below the upper border as that between the pinholes, and the same distance being left between the sides and their nearest pinholes. This distance between the pinholes is regulated by the length of the leaves.

Sets of four bobbins are hung along the upper border, at points above each pinhole. Each set is worked with four or more stitches as desired (No. 3A, p. 102); each pair being twisted, supported on a pin and left.

A set of four bobbins is next hung on the left side a little below the level of the pins just set, and the same number of leaf stitches made with them as with the upper sets. The side set is then worked through the first upper set (twists being made before and after each stitch), another leaf made as directed above, the next set worked through, and this repeated to the end of the row. The side set is then sewn into the right side at the correct level, twisted, and sewn again ready for the next row of pinholes. The upper sets are again worked, the side set worked back, and this repeated till the space is filled. It is important that the correct number of twists should be made with each pair used before and after each stitch.

6. **Leaves and Crosses.**—This is made in the same way as No. 4, till the end of the first row. For the second row, take one pair from the right and one from the left leaves, which should have been already twisted three times. Make a whole stitch with them and twist each pair three times.

For the third row, beginning with a pair sewn into the side from the first row and the nearest twisted pair from the upper sets, work leaves as in the first row. This will pull the twisted threads into place and show the crosses.

The rows are worked alternately, one of leaves· and one of crosses.

As in all leaf fillings the shapes may be Square, Oval, Beehive or Hour-glass.

7. **Double-set Chequered Leaf.**—If the pattern be pricked on paper ruled with twenty-five squares to the inch, in the first row leave one square between the first and second pinhole, and five between the second and third, and so alternately throughout the row. Leave one row of squares between every two rows of pinholes. The second row is like the first, with each pinhole directly under another.

In the third row, number the square under the first pinhole as one, and make the first pinhole in the fifth square. One square is left between the first and second pinholes and five between the second and third. This is repeated alternately to the end of the row. The fourth row has its pinholes directly under those of the third.

The rest of the pattern is pricked in the same manner, the fifth and sixth being like the first and second, and seventh and eighth like the third and fourth, etc.

The bobbins are hung in double sets (of four pairs), between each pair of pinholes, *i.e.* with a pair of pinholes between each double set, in the first row ; a single set of two pairs only being hung at each end of the row.

Take the two pairs at the extreme left, twist each pair three times and make a cloth stitch, setting a pin between the pairs in the first pinhole on the left.

Take the two left-hand pairs from the next set and twist each pair three times, make a cloth stitch and set a pin between the pairs in the second pinhole on the left.

There will now be two pairs from each pin, making still a set of four. Of these, the two inner pairs will be used to make a leaf and the two outer pairs will make a twisted loop running down the outside of it. Twist the outer pairs each three times and make a leaf with the two middle pairs. Stitch the left middle and outside pairs, set a pin between them in the left pinhole of the second row, and twist each pair three times. Repeat with the two right-hand pairs. The first leaf is now complete, and the others are made in the same way.

The second row is made from two pairs from each of the adjoining first row sets and leaves the two end pairs disengaged. Each of these must be twisted and sewn into the side, at the level of the upper pinholes of the second row, then twisted, and sewn again level with its lower pinhole.

The succeeding rows will be alternately like the first and second.

The leaves may be either of the four shapes.

8. **Double-set Leaf and Cross.**—The pattern for this, if pricked on square ruled paper about twenty-five to the inch, should have the first and second pinholes separated by one unused square. Three squares are missed between the second and third pinholes and the rest of the row is pricked alternately in the same manner. One row of squares is left unused between every two rows of pinholes.

The second row is like the first, with every pinhole placed directly under one in the first row.

In the third row the first pinhole is pricked in the fifth square, counting that under the first pinhole of the upper rows as one. Five squares are left unused between every two pinholes of this row. This should place the pinholes under the middle square of the three missed in the first and second rows.

The fourth and fifth rows will be like the first and second, and the sixth like the third, and so alternately to the end of the space. Two rows of pinholes are used for each row of leaves.

The first row of the working is like No. 7, but in the second row the sets, which in No. 7 would be used to make new leaves, are worked through each other, and twisted ready for the next row.

For this, take the two right-hand pairs from one set and the two left-hand pairs from its neighbour. The two middle pairs make a cloth stitch and a pin is set between them, in the nearest hole of the third row. Next make cloth stitches between the two left- and two right-hand pairs. Enclose the pin by a stitch between the two middle pairs and twist every pair three times.

The rows are alternately like the first and the second. Sewings are made in a line with the pinholes for the second and alternate rows. The leaves may be of either of the four shapes.

9. **Double-set Leaves and Flowers.**—This is worked on the same pattern as above, and the first row made in the same way, but with no twisting after the leaf is made. These single leaves should be as large and well filled as possible.

In the second row a small oval leaf is made with the two pairs taken from the left set and another with the two from the right. The sets are then worked through each other as above and another leaf formed with each set. This completes the four-petaled flower.

The rows are alternately alike.

The double-set leaves may be of either of the four shapes, but a more floral effect is given by a rather long oval.

To accentuate this, two rows of squares may be left unused between the first and second and corresponding rows.

Variations in the distance between the pinholes in each row may also be made if preferred.

**10. Double-set Leaf and Trellis.**—This is made on the same pattern as No. 8 (p. 107) and the first row is worked like No. 7 (p. 106).

In the second row, sew the extreme left- and extreme right-hand bobbins to their sides, making them level with those pinholes which are provided for the trellis-work in the second row. Leave those pairs which are next to the left and right hanging ready for use in the third row, each pair being twisted three times.

Take the right-hand pair from the first set on the left, and the left-hand pair from its neighbour. Twist each pair, make half-stitch, and set a pin between the bobbins in the nearest pinhole of the second row. Make another half-stitch and give each pair two extra twists, making three, with that left by the half-stitch.

Repeat with the right and left pairs of each set.

The inner pairs of the first row are not used in the second row, but left to hang and form the outer boundary of the trellis.

Further rows are alternately like the first and second.

The leaves may be of either of the four shapes.

**11. Double-set Leaf and Double Trellis.**—This is made on the same pattern as No. 8, and the working begun in the same way as No. 7 : but when the first leaf on the left has been made, the outside pair on the left is twisted three times, and sewn to the edge at the level of the centre of the leaf. It is then again twisted three times and cloth-stitched with the next pair on the left. A pin is then set between the pairs in the left-hand lower pinhole of the first leaf. Both pairs are then twisted and the outside pair sewn to the side level with the holes made for the trellis of the second row and twisted again. The inner pair will be left hanging ready for the third row.

The leaf second on the left is now made and its left-outside pair twisted three times and cloth-stitched with the right-hand pair from the left set, also twisted three times. After the stitch both pairs are again twisted, completing the work for the extra trellis.

The extra trellis pair on the left is now cloth-stitched with the next pair on its left and a pin set between the pairs in the right-hand lower pinhole of the first leaf, both pairs being twisted and left. The right-hand pair of the trellis is next stitched with the left-hand pair of the second leaf, a pin is set between the pairs and both are twisted and left.

The rest of the row is made in the same way.

Two leaves must be worked before one trellis can be made, as the trellis lying between them is made by the exchange of their outside pairs.

The second row is made in the same way as the corresponding row in No. 10 (p. 108).

The leaves may be of either of the four shapes.

12. **Basket.**—This requires the support of leaf-stitch pins (p. 13).

Hang two pairs of bobbins in the middle pinhole of the upper border of the space in which the basket is to be made. These form the handle ; twist each pair six or more times, and lay them down.

Hang one pair at the right- and left-hand edges of the space being filled, which should be little larger than the basket, on a level with its top.

There are now eight threads provided. Take seven leaf pins and stick them on the cushion about 6 in. below the basket, well spread out and at even distances from each other. Lay the two threads on the left, each into the circle of the pin to which it seems to belong.

Do the same for the two threads and pins on the right.

Of the two middle pairs, take the left-hand bobbin as a weaver, and place the others each in the circle to which, in position, it belongs.

Pass the weaving bobbin under the thread next it on the right, and over and under the others to the extreme right bobbin, which it first passes under, and then commences the next row by passing over.

If the space should require it, extra pairs of bobbins may be hung on separate pins along the upper edge of the basket, which will be woven through as the weavers come to them. (See Fig. 82.)

Weave over and under the threads in this way, tightening and loosening to shape the basket, till it is large enough.

Take the threads from the leaf pins, and remove the pins.

Make three half-stitches with the four left-hand bobbins, and three with the four right-hand ones. Or if extra bobbins have been used, divide the total number in two or three sets as may be preferred and make three half-stitches with each set. Lay the bobbins together evenly in the centre and work a piece of double stem stitch nearly long enough to reach the lower border of the space.

Twist each pair three times and sew to the lower border, spreading the pairs out evenly to make a foot for the stand of the basket. Tie and cut off (p. 32).

A simpler way is to make the basket of the right size to rest on the lower border, when each pair may be crossed, sewn and cut off ; or may be twisted a few times, spread out to make a foot, sewn, and cut off.

13. **Cobwebs with Six Strands.**—Mark six places round the border of the space to be filled, so arranged that the threads will

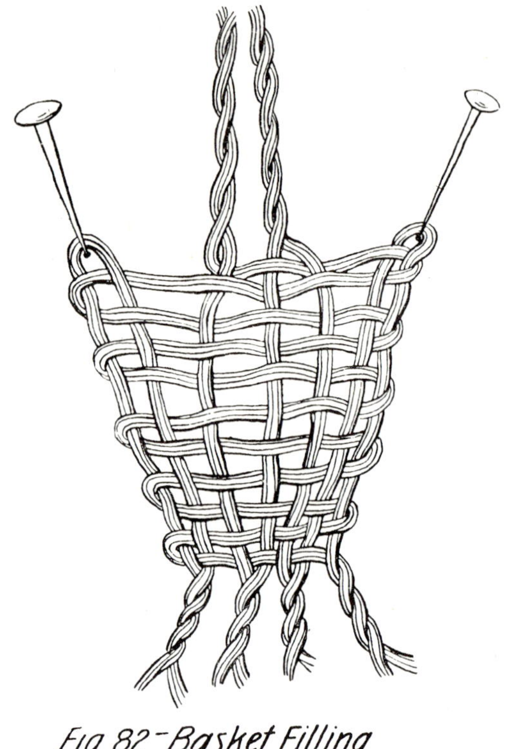

Fig 82 — Basket Filling

lie at equal distances from each other when radiating from the centre of the circle ; the place for which must also be marked.

Hang a pair of bobbins at each of the three upper marks and twist each pair six times. Make a half-stitch with the two left-hand pairs, the same with the two right-hand ones and again with the left set. Place a pin in the centre with three bobbins on either side, make a half-stitch with the two right pairs, another with the two left, and yet one more with the two right. Twist six times, tie, and cut off. (See Fig. 83.)

The following method is simpler, but has a less finished appearance.  After the three pairs are hung and twisted, make a whole stitch with the two pairs on the left and set a pin between them in the centre hole.  Make a whole stitch with the right-hand pairs and another with the left.  Twist, sew, and cut off (p. 32).

14. **Cobwebs with Eight Strands.**—Mark eight places (as in No. 13, p. 110).

Hang four pairs of bobbins, one at each of the upper marks and twist each pair six times.

Make a cloth stitch between the two centre pairs, and the same

Fig. 83 - Cobweb with Six Strands

between the two pairs on the left and on the right.  Make another stitch between the two centre pairs and set a pin between them.  Another stitch is now made between the two pairs, both on the left and right :  and one more between the two centre pairs. Twist each pair six times, sew into place, tie, and cut off (p. 32).

The number of bobbins used for a cobweb is optional, and naturally the greater the number the larger the centre.

An even number of pairs may have the centre of whole stitch, but an uneven number goes better in half-stitch.

15. **Cross Strands for Cobwebs.**—If cross strands be desired on a cobweb commenced in the ordinary way from the borders of the space to be filled, all the strands but one must be sewn to their places and tied, after the centre is worked.

The pair left unsewn is taken for weaving, a pin being first set

at every strand at the place where the cross strand intersects it.
The weavers are twisted enough for their own distance from the
centre and also for one space between the strands ; they are
passed outside their pin from the right and twisted and sewn to
the strands in succession.   At the return of the weavers to their
original place they are sewn into their own strand close to the
pin.   Further cross strands are worked in same way, the distances
between them being greater as the circumference increases.
When the cross strands are finished the weavers are sewn, tied,
and cut off.   (See Fig. 84.)
In strands of four or more threads, it is better to take but one

Fig. 84—Cobweb with Cross Strands

pair as weavers, which will be twisted and sewn as usual, returning to plait into their strand when they touch it again.

16. **Cobweb from Centre.**—The pattern for this has a centre
pinhole, and if cross strands are desired, must have a pinhole for
each place where the cross strands touch the straight ones.
The pinholes for each cross strand must be at even distances
from the centre.   (See Fig. 85.)
Round the border of the space to be filled mark the same
number of places as there are pairs of bobbins in use.   This
number should be even, and not less than six.   Place two pins
close to the centre pinhole, to the left and right.
Lay a pair of bobbins with the thread between the pins, with
one bobbin on either side of the pillow.   Lay the other pairs,

one at a time, beside it ; so that the threads shall not cross, and that each pair shall lie over the pinholes made for its cross strands. The two pins may be withdrawn after the weavers have made one round, but one pin must then be set in the centre hole.

Take a pair of bobbins, lying on the right-hand side of a pin, as weavers, and work round the other bobbins to the left in whole stitch till the centre is as large as desired and the weavers are in the place from which they started. Sew the weavers to the thread of the last row to keep them in place.

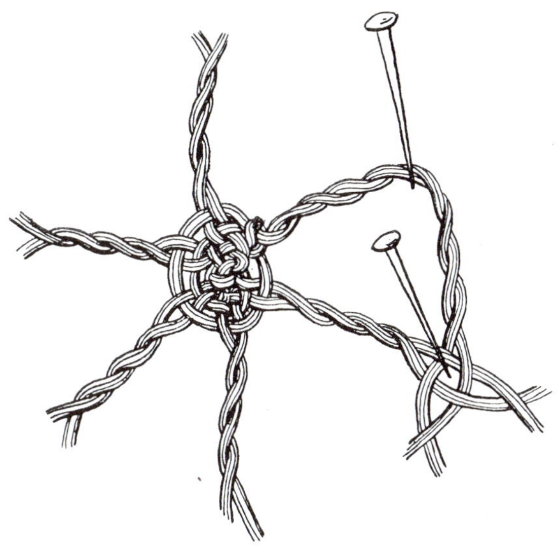

Fig. 85 — Cobweb from Centre

If no cross strands are to be used, each strand may now be twisted, as required, sewn in its place, tied, and cut off.

If there be cross strands, place a pin in the hole nearest the centre along the weaver's line (for its strand). Keep the weavers to the right of this pin and twist them nine times. Twist the other pairs each three times. Of course, the number of all these twists may be increased if desired.

Make a half-stitch between the weavers and the next pair on the left, and set a pin between the pair in the next cross-strand pinhole. Make another half-stitch and twist the weavers five times (which, with the half-stitch cross, makes six twists). Work round with the weavers in this way, making a half-stitch with each pair, setting a pin between the pairs, enclosing with another

H

half-stitch and giving the weavers six twists between each two pins.

When the weavers arrive at the place from which they started, after they have been twisted, they are sewn to their own strand at the place where the pin was set.

If further cross strands are arranged, they are made in the same way, the number of times the weavers are twisted increasing as the distance between the pins becomes greater.   The distance and number of twists between the cross strands should increase also as they are placed further from the centre.

When the cross strands are finished, the bars are twisted, sewn, tied, and cut off (p. 32).

17. **Cobweb with Coronet and Picots.**—This looks best with a cobweb of at least six strands in not too small a space.

All bars but one must be finished, sewn, and tied.

For plaited strands, set a pin on the line of the unfinished bar, at a short distance from the centre spot, which the coronet should touch, but not overlap.   Work a piece of bar of a length to reach the pin, keeping the bar on the right of the latter.

Taking the number of stitches between the bars to be six and that there are to be two picots between them, then two pinholes are made between each two bars, at even distances from each other, remembering that the picots must be on the outside of the coronet.

Work two stitches, make a picot on the right-hand side of the bar, setting the pin in the nearest hole.   Make two more stitches, another picot, yet two other stitches and sew into the next bar. Make another stitch and sew again on the opposite side of the bar.

Work all round in the same way, sewing carefully to the bars and taking care that the bar and threads are not dragged.

When the coronet reaches the starting-point, sew into its left edge just above the pin, make a stitch, sew again, finish the strand, sew, tie, and cut off.

With twisted bars of two threads hang on an extra pair of bobbins over a pin when commencing the coronet, withdrawing the pin and pulling up its loop after two stitches.

18. **Snake Centre.**—The pattern for this has a pinhole in the centre, and, starting from this, other pinholes wind round and round from left to right like a shell or Catherine-wheel till they complete the circumference at a convenient point for tying off.

Hang four pairs of bobbins upon a pin in the centre hole.   Make the ordinary edge at the side furthest from the centre and work the other in stem stitch, from which frequent sewings should be made into convenient loops as soon as the first circle is completed.

For a snake effect increase in width by adding occasional

bobbins till near the middle ; and decrease by throwing them off as the tail is worked.

For a shell, keep the first rounds small, then continually increase to the finish, which must be finished off to look like the mouth of the shell, and tied off strongly (p. 32).

19. **Crossed Bars : Picots at Centre.**—One or more picots may be set in the angle of each bar.  They look best made with thick pins and standing well out.

With two sets of four bobbins work two bars in half-stitch to their meeting-point (say at right angles).  At the upper angle make a picot with a pair from one bar and finish it with a pair from the other.  Pull up well, and make one stitch with the left and another with the right sets of bobbins.  (See Fig. 86.)

Fig. 86 — Cross Bars Picots at Centre

The outside pair on the left makes the picot on that side, and the other pair from the left is used to finish it.

The right-hand picot is made by the outside pair on the right, and finished by a stitch of the two right-hand pairs.

The last picot must be made with care.  Take the right-hand pair from the left-hand set, twist it six times and make a picot. Place the picot bobbins on the pillow, a little to the left of the left-hand bar.  Take the left-hand pair from the right-hand bar and, passing them behind the picot pin, lay them on the left of the picot bobbins.  Make a cloth stitch between them to finish the picot.  Take the pair now on the left of the two middle bobbins, pass them behind the picot pin, and lay them as the left-hand pair of the right-hand bar.  Take the next pair on the left and place them as the right-hand pair of the left-hand bar.  Make a few stitches first with one bar and then with the other, pull up well, finish the bars and tie off (p. 32).

20. **Bar Squares or Diamonds.**—Hang on the bobbins for each bar in groups equidistant from each other (p. 75).

Hang a set also at one side, at the same distance from the top that the groups are from each other.

Work the upper sets in half-stitch till they are long enough to meet the cross bar, making the same number of stitches with each, and work the side bar for the same number of stitches as the upper sets.

Work the pairs from the side bar through the first upper bar in cloth stitch ; and again make the same number of half-stitches as with the upper sets. When the bar has been worked across, it must be sewn to the edge and be then tied and cut off : or each pair may be twisted and brought down the edge, to the place for the next side bar.

For diamond-shaped spaces, hang one bar on either side of a corner, and arrange each bar to run parallel with the opposite side ; hanging further bars on either side as required.

21A. **Honeycomb Bars.**—Eight bobbins in each set are hung at equal distances along the upper border of the space. A pair of the left-hand set is taken as weavers and eight rows (more or less) are worked in double stem stitch. This is repeated with each set in the row.

In the second row each set is divided. The four bobbins on the left are worked eight times, sewn into the side, worked eight times again, and again sewn : then worked eight times more and left. Next, one set of four from the first set, and one from the second, are separately worked each eight times and then placed together, one pair taken as weavers and eight rows worked. The rest of the row is worked in the same way, the last set of four on the right being worked and sewn into the side, as was done for the left-hand ones.

This is handsome when well planned : as a partial grounding it contrasts well with Lille net. Made with fine thread and few stitches, it makes a beautiful filling for flower centres, medallions, etc.

21B. **Bars with Picots.**—These are made in the same way as the plain ones of the various shapes, but with picots added at regular intervals, usually on one side only of the bar. With the honeycomb shape picots may be placed at regular distances inside each cell or in alternate cells, and this in each or in alternate rows.

22. **Spots.**—These may be worked on a ground of most kinds of net, or at the junction of two or more bars.

In the case of net the places must be marked on the pattern and clothwork or a leaf worked there of the shape required (p. 101).

In preparing a pattern for spots, where bars cross, place a pin-hole at the centre of crossing and pinholes for each side in the positions proper for the size and shape of the clothwork spot.

If a spot is desired at the crossing of two twisted bars larger than would be made by their working through each other in cloth stitch, make a half-stitch between the two pairs, at their junction, give an extra twist to one pair and set a pin close to their crossing-place.   Make another half-stitch, give an extra twist to the pair on the other side and set a pin between the pairs on the same side as the twist.

Another half-stitch, extra twist and pin is now made for each side, and the bars are completed, or continued, to the next crossing.   The pins should be set close to the crossing and close together.

If the bars are plaited and so consist of four or more bobbins, one of the middle pairs is taken for weaving (say from the right-hand set), worked across to the left and then backwards and forwards in cloth stitch, two twists being made and a pin set between the weavers and warps at each side before the weavers return.   When the spot is large enough, the weavers are left as the inner pair of the set other than the one from which they were taken.   The bars are then completed, or continued to the next crossing.

A lighter appearance may be given by extra twists, when the pins are set, or by making a picot with each pin.

23. **Chessboard in Linen Stitch.** — This filling requires no pattern.

Hang four pairs of bobbins on the upper border of the space to be filled, leave the space for four more, and hang four others : repeating this to the end of the row.   Twist each pair six or more times.   Hang a pair of weavers on one of the sides at the distance of the space for four pairs, and twist as many times as has been done for the upper pairs, if the upper row be finished by a space ; but if the upper row be finished by a set of bobbins, the weavers will require no twisting.   (See Fig. 87.)

Work through the first set of four in cloth stitch, or fancy, if preferred, twist the same number of times as before, and repeat to the end of the row.   Sew into the side at the level of the first row to finish it ; and at the level of the second row ready to begin it. These rows must be as distant from each other as the pairs in the upper row.   Three more rows, four in all, are worked in the same way.   Then, after sewing the weavers to complete the row, they are twisted and sewn again at the distance between the upper sets.

The upper bobbins are twisted as before, and four more rows worked.   This is repeated until the space is filled.

24. **Diamonds in Linen Stitch.**—Along the upper border of the space to be filled alternately hang on four pairs of bobbins and (between each set and at the beginning and end of each row) miss

a like space to that taken up by the four pairs. Arrange the threads of each set diagonally across the space from right to left. Hang another set on the right border, beginning close to the top. Miss a like space and hang another set and continue this alternately down the side till there are enough sets to fill the ground to be occupied, when placed diagonally, as alternate lines and spaces.

These bobbin threads are the warps. They are traversed diagonally in the opposite direction by a pair of weavers that

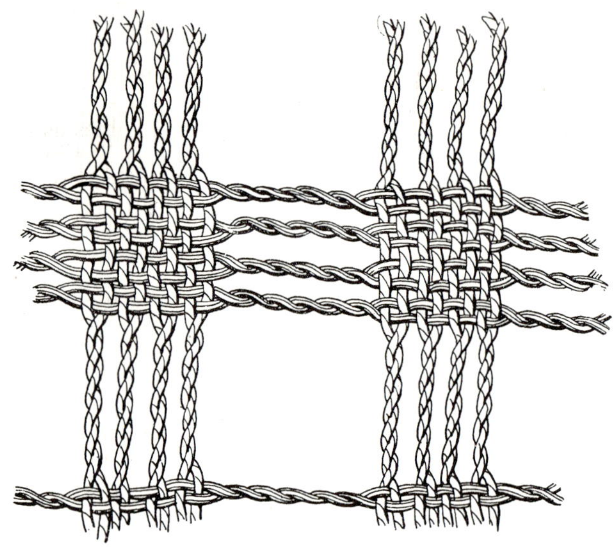

Fig. 87 — Chessboard in Linen-stitch

alternately work four lines and miss the space of four. (See Fig. 88.)

Hang a pair of weavers just below the upper set of side bobbins. Cross them once, cross the nearest pair of side bobbins above them and work the weavers through them in cloth stitch. Cross the next pair respectively twice, four times and six times, work the weavers through the three pairs and twist them six times. Then work through the first pair of the nearest set on the upper border and sew to the upper edge, between the first and second pairs dependent from it. Cross the weavers once and sew again between the second and third pairs. Work the weavers through the second and first pairs of the upper set, twist six times, work through the

four side pairs, twist twice, and sew to the side.  Cross the
weavers, sew again, twist four times, work through the next four
pairs, twist six times, work through three pairs and sew to the
upper edge.  Cross and sew again on the left of the fourth pair,
work through the four bobbins, twist six times, work through
again to the side, twist six times and sew.

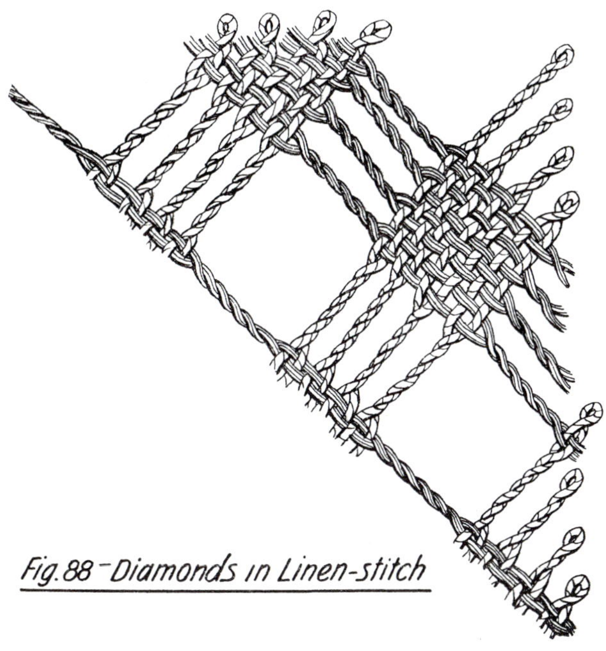

Fig. 88 — Diamonds in Linen-stitch

Twist the weavers six times and sew them just below the second
set of four at the side.   Twist the bobbins already worked through
six times.

Work the weavers through as before : every row must have
thought and care.  The sets must be sewn to suitable places
when worked enough, and may need twisting first from two to
six times.

This is a filling more suited to experts than beginners.

# CHAPTER XII

# SPECIAL KINDS OF LACE

**D**EVONIAN.—The main part of this lace, the background, so to speak, is made in the ordinary way : but petals of flowers and any parts of other ornaments that will lend themselves to the treatment, are made on separate patterns and afterwards sewn upon the underwork, so that they stand up in relief upon a flat background of lace.

For these flowers, invisible hanging on will be found most useful, almost necessary.

As an example : The stem and calyx of a water-lily, with its bold sepals, may be made in the usual way. The petals are next made on a separate pattern and sewn on ; and lastly, the stamens are also made and sewn into place. Thus the flower stands up with a striking and distinctive effect. For artistic reasons the method should be used with restraint.

Naturally, this lace will require unusual care in cleaning.

**Skeleton Leaf.**—In the hands of an expert, this lace should be quickly worked and very effective. It may be made up without a ground or mounted on net, fine and good. Unmounted, it has a good effect on dark velvet or a rich dark silk.

The patterns require only single lines of pinholes.

The outlines and principal veins and stems may be worked in single or double stem stitch, with few bobbins and fine thread, while smaller veins may be put in with plaited bars of four threads and the very smallest in twisted ones.

The pins should be set rather close together, and the work well pulled up. Sewings may be avoided to some extent by hanging on bobbins for the veins along the outline, at places where they are marked and working them down to the mid-rib, in which they may be incorporated, too great thickness being avoided by throwing back superfluous bobbins from time to time.

Picots should be freely used.

Sewings and fastenings must be neat and strong.


## NEEDLE POINT.

This, when correctly made, is, perhaps, the most beautiful and valuable of all laces : but in England, its name has been taken

NEEDLEPOINT BORDERS: ITALIAN.   17th Cent.
*(In the Victoria and Albert Museum.)*

[*face p.* 120

for an inferior class of lace, and its reputation has suffered accordingly, with those who have not studied the subject.

In the, practically valueless, imitation " Point," several kinds of braid are used, with which to make a superficial resemblance to the clothwork of Duchesse and Bruges ; and to these are often added fillings and grounds of genuine Needle Point stitches, with a somewhat bizarre effect.

The use of these braids is a grave mistake, for the genuine lace is not difficult to make, and by using only thread and cord to mark the outlines, the value of the work is multiplied many times.

Patterns should be traced on thin white or green paper and pasted or sewn to stout paper, fine American cloth, or toile cirée, which is to be obtained at most needlework repositories. The outlines are then pricked as for Honiton (p. 38).

Point de Gaze, or Point d'Alençon may be the easiest variety for a beginner. Venetian Point is heavy, and Rose Point rather too elaborate for any one person to hope to make more than a small piece in the time which most people can give to it.

Whatever the style chosen, either a clear picture or a piece of the lace in question should be obtained, and a pattern, properly traced, mounted and perforated.

Thread, single or doubled as many times as desired, or a suitable cord must now be traced along every outline, and fixed in place by passing frequent stitches over it, the needle going in and out of the same hole, the outline being perforated for that purpose.

A stitch called Point d'Entoilage, or Linen Point, is largely used in the place of the Linen Stitch of Honiton and Brussels, and the worker's first task is to fill the appointed parts with this.

Both this and all subsequent work must be done with care, neither to make any part too loosely, so as to form anything approaching a bulge above the general flat surface, nor to strain any part so that the outline is disturbed.

It must be remembered that Needle Point, unlike Honiton, Brussels, etc., is worked right side out ; so that all commencements and fastenings must be invisible from the upper side.

The stem and the heavier parts of the design may be worked in the supported Brussels Stitch, mentioned above as Point d'Entoilage, closer or more open, according to the character of the work and of the particular portion of the pattern in hand. Other parts, such as petals, shields, cornucopias, etc., may be put in with suitable fancy stitches ; the centres of flowers and other small finishings being treated elaborately.

Having finished the interior of the sprigs, etc., throughout the work, the grounding of net or bars must be added.

For Point de Gaze, the ground must be net ; for Point de

Venise, bars.  Alençon is grounded with net, as a whole, but in certain parts has bar fillings in elaborately minute detail.

Having made and grounded the lace, proceed to cover the outlines with even button-hole stitches, in a manner suited to the character of the lace.  The edges may be smooth or enriched by loops, etc., according to the style chosen.

It is quite possible for a clever needlewoman to make a beautiful lace in Needle Point without a sample to copy, but no one can expect to imitate a given style in that way.

If Point de—Anything is to be produced, obtain first a clear picture, or photograph, of it, if the lace itself is not obtainable ; and note every detail, however small.  Then carry out your work ;  not imitating slavishly, but seizing and reproducing the special characteristics of the lace.

Brussels and Honiton are made by variations of Linen Stitch, and Needle Point has also one stitch by means of which its varied

Fig. 89 - Tulle -stitch

beauties are elaborated.  This is the simple Button-hole Stitch.

This stitch is used in very various ways, plain, patterns of alternated closeness, duplicated in various ways, twisted, and supported by extra threads.

The stitches are numerous, but if a few of the principal varieties are given, the student can, from them, work out many others.

First, there is the plain Button-hole worked at even distances across the space to be filled on the outlining thread.  (See Fig. 89.)  At the end of the row one overcasting stitch is made on the outlining thread to finish the row, and another to begin a new one.  For the after rows, stitches are made into each mesh of the preceding one.

It is better to count the number of stitches in the first row and to see that each succeeding one has the same number.  Otherwise it is not always clear where to set the first and last stitches of the row.  This is called Tulle Stitch or Point de Tulle, and is the ground chiefly used in Point de Gaze, Duchesse, and many other laces.

It may be varied by putting the point of the needle when it comes through the mesh over the thread and then through the mesh again, making a double twist. This, which we may call double Tulle Stitch, is used sometimes instead of No. 4. (See Fig. 90.)

After Tulle, the stitch of most importance is a variation made

*Fig. 90 — Double Tulle-stitch*

by passing a thread before commencing and after the end of each row across to the side where the first row is started. (See Fig. 91.) The line is fastened in place by the usual stitches, and in the succeeding row the needle takes up the thread line with its stitch into each mesh.

Point d'Entoilage, or Linen Stitch, is the name of this ground.

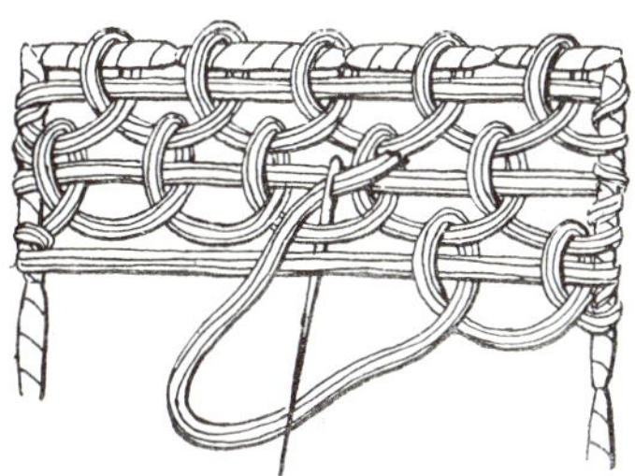

*Fig. 91 — Point d'Entoilage*

It is used for stems, leaves, and any of the simpler parts of the design.

The ground of Point d'Alençon is a variation in another direction and is known as Point Feston Doublé. (See Fig. 92.) In the ordinary button-hole stitch, the point of the needle takes up the thread of a mesh of the last made row, and passes inside the mesh it is making. In Point d'Alençon the needle commences at the left, takes up the mesh as above, but emerges first outside the one being made, then passes inside it and then out again. Further, at the end of the row, the needle is sewn three times into

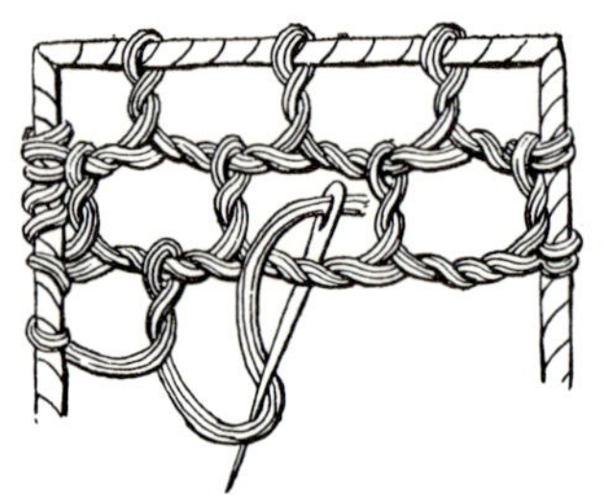

Fig. 92 - Point Feston Double

each mesh on its return to the left side, at which each row begins. This ground should be made with exceedingly fine thread. It is sometimes worked backward and forward without sewing over.

Another useful stitch is made on an ordinary Button-hole Stitch carefully pulled up, by making a second like stitch into the

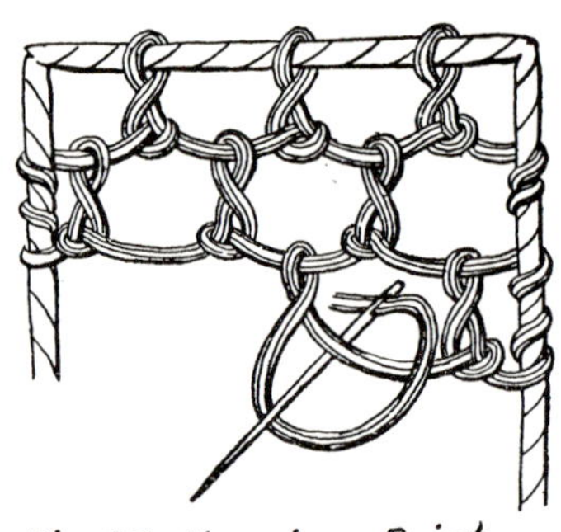

Fig. 93 - Venetian Point

one just made, taking up one thread. This is much used in Venetian Point and may be called by its name, Point de Venise. (See Fig. 93.)

A variation on this is to place the second stitch in the middle of the first mesh and follow it by making several others across the doubled threads.   The stitch is known as Point de Grain or Corn Stitch.   (See Fig. 94.)

A further variety, Point de Filet, or Net Stitch, consists in making a second Button-hole Stitch across *both* threads of the

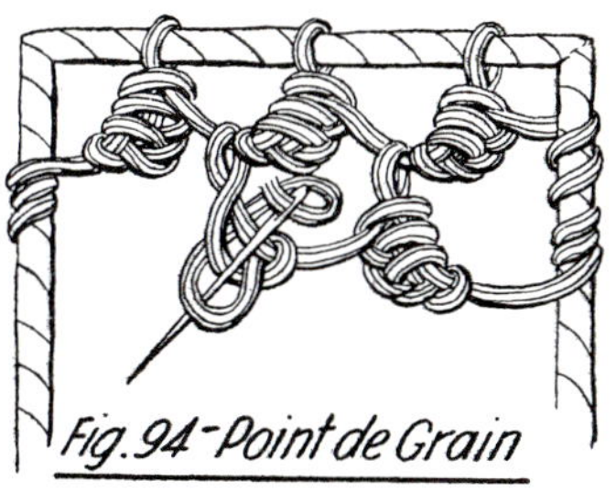


first.   (See Fig. 95.)   This, commenced across a corner, and worked backwards and forwards, is used for a strong ground which looks like netting.

For bars in Needle Point there are the twisted, the button-hole, and a basketwork kind ;  and each may or may not be decorated with picots of various styles.

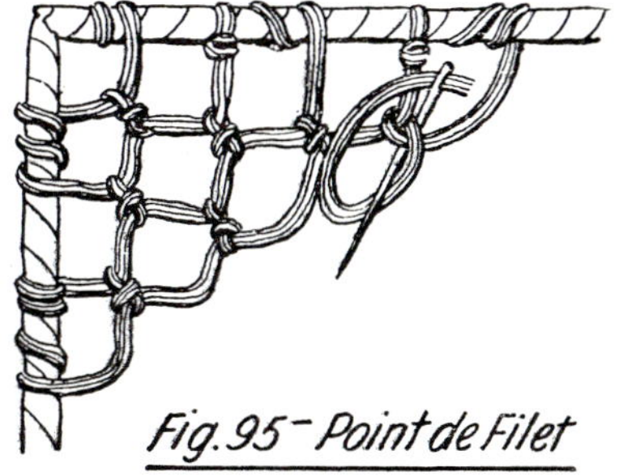

The twisted bar consists of a thread fastened across a space with a return thread sewn round it and finished at the point where the first one started.   This is used in making cobwebs, etc.   (See Fig. 96.)

For cobwebs the first thread is stretched across and fastened, the return thread being sewn back to the centre, making an even twist ;  and new strands are started from there, carried to the edge, sewn over to the centre and continued to the spot opposite their starting-point.   The return thread is sewn back to the

centre as before and another strand started. (See Fig. 97.)
When enough strands have been started, pass the needle under

Fig. 97—Cobweb Ordinary

one thread and over another, round and round, till the cobweb

Fig. 98—Cobweb Raised Rib

is of the size required. Finish on the single strand, sew over it
to the edge, and fasten off neatly and securely.

Instead of darning in and out round the cobweb, the needle may be brought out on the left of a strand, passed over it and under both it and the strand next on the left. As before, it

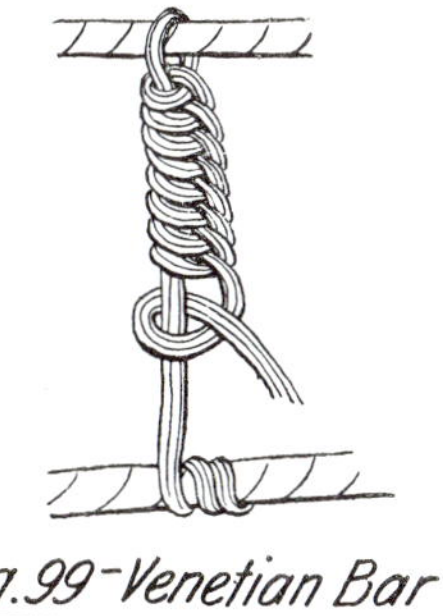

Fig. 99 - Venetian Bar

emerges on the left of the second strand and is passed over it, and under it and its left-hand neighbour. (See Fig. 98.) This is continued till the centre is large enough, when the cobweb is finished as before.

Fig. 100 - Venetian Cobweb

The button-holed or Venetian bar is managed in the same way as the twisted one, but a row of button-hole stitches, instead of twists, is used to finish it. (See Fig. 99.)

If the Venetian bars should be used for a cobweb, a circle at the centre should be made by passing a thread over and under the strands and then covered with button-holing. (See Fig. 100.)

The Venetian bars are also used for an irregular ground, by making the net first of Tulle or Feston (p. 122) on a large open scale, and afterwards covering it with button-holing.  (See Fig. 101.)

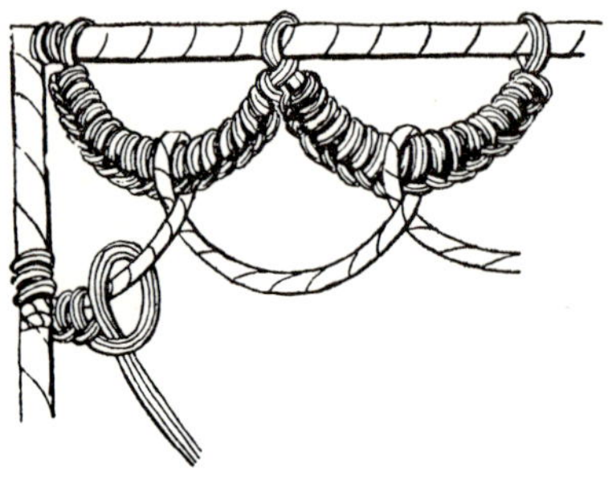

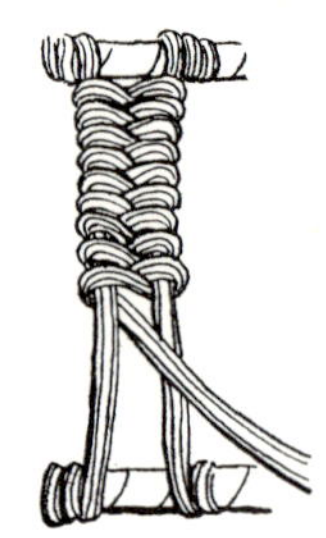

Fig. 101 ‑ Venetian Bar Ground.        Fig. 102 ‑ Reprise Bar

The basketwork, or Reprise bar, is made by stretching two or more threads across a space, and passing the needle over one and under the other, till the bar is covered with even stitches.  (See Fig. 102.)

Fig. 103 ‑ French Knot

A picot may be made on a twisted bar by passing the needle partly under the bar, winding the thread several times round it, pushing the needle through and pulling up the thread with care. This is called a French knot.  (See Fig. 103.)

On a Venetian bar a Venetian Loop picot may be made by passing the thread round a pin, stuck near the bar, before the button-hole stitch is pulled up : then tightening it and making another button-hole stitch over its three threads close to the bar. (See Fig. 104.)

Another method is to fill the space between the pin and the bar with button-hole stitches. This is a typical Venetian picot. (See Fig. 105.)

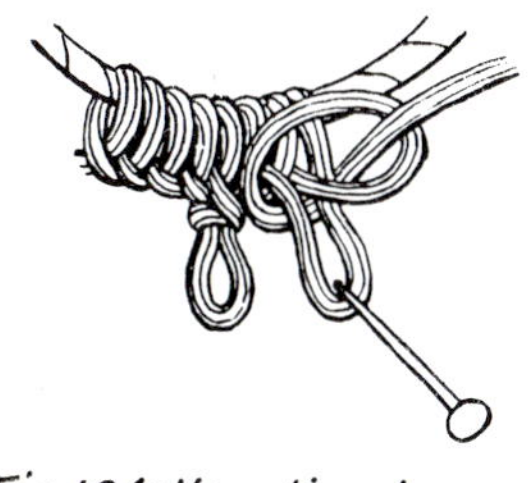

Fig. 104 - Venetian Loop

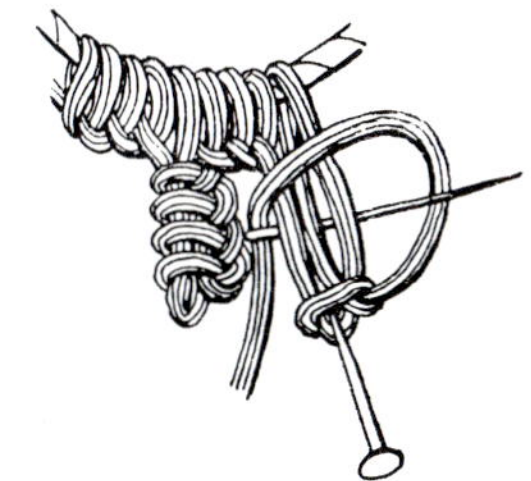

Fig. 105 - Venetian Picot

A Rose Point Loop may be made by taking a stitch back, a little way, upon the part of the bar just made, and filling it with button-hole stitches. (See Fig. 106.)

Yet other picots, French Eyelets, are made by passing the needle half-way through the bar, winding the thread many times round it, pulling it through and fixing it in place. (See Fig. 107.)

Rosettes are worked on many kinds of net by making a very

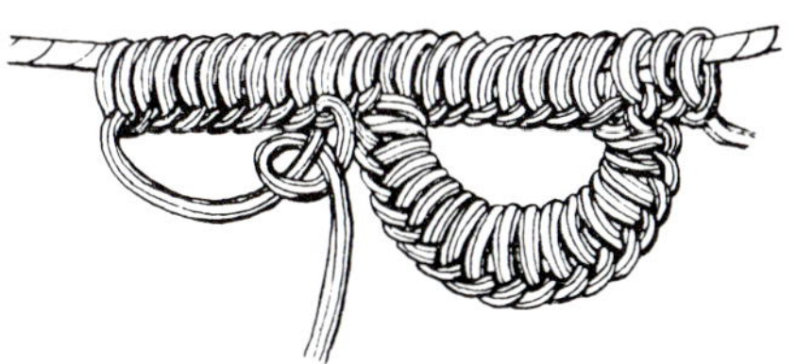

Fig. 106 - Rose Point Loop

small circle of thread on the ground and covering it with button-hole stitches. (See Fig. 108.)

Other spots are made by sewing some four parallel stitches over several rows of net ; the stitches going in and out at the same places or spreading slightly. The French name for these is Mouches. We may perhaps know them as Bees. (See Fig. 109.)

Edges are made ornamental by using a single row of numbers, Tulle, Venise Grain, or possibly Feston. Rose Point edge is made by throwing back two loops, one behind the other, filling the one furthest back with button-hole stitches continued half-way over the second.   Another loop is now thrown back to the centre of the furthest one, and filled with the button-holing, which is continued over the unfinished half of the lower loop.   (See Fig. 110.)   This edge may be adorned with picots of various kinds.

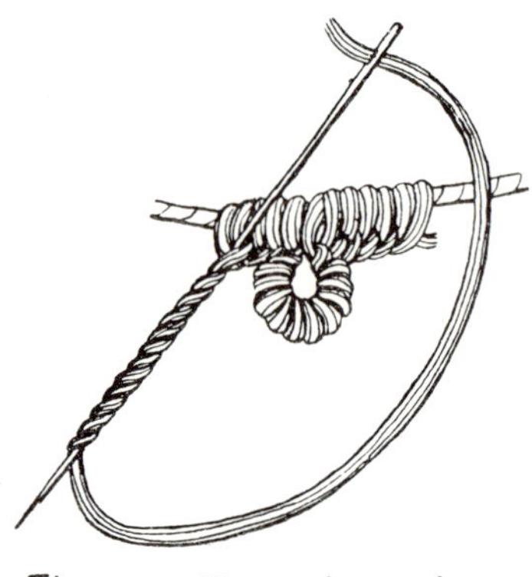

Fig. 107 — French Eyelets

With several of the foregoing stitches, such as Tulle, Feston or Venise, patterns may be made as follows, for example :—For a perforated network, say, two stitches close together, miss the space of two and repeat.   In the next row, put two stitches into the long loops and one into the short.   The third row will repeat the first, and the fourth the second.   This may, of course, be much varied.   (See Fig. 111.)

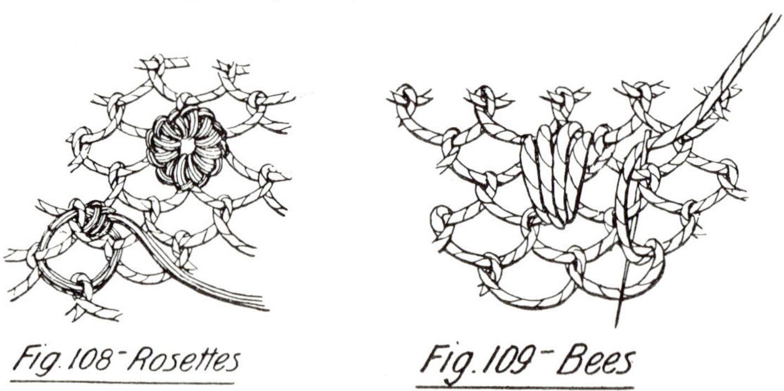

Fig. 108 — Rosettes          Fig. 109 — Bees

For another style, the **V**-ground, make four close stitches, miss one and repeat to the end of the row.   In the next row, set three stitches into the loops of the four and repeat.   The third row, two stitches into the loops of the three and repeat.   And for the

fourth row one stitch into the loop between the two.  In the
fifth row four stitches are made into each long loop, and the pro-

Fig. 110 - Rose Point Edge

cess repeated, reversing the position of the close and open work.
(See Fig. 112.)

By varying the number of stitches set close together and the
length of spaces, a further great variety of patterns may be produced.   Both this and the foregoing patterns may multiply their

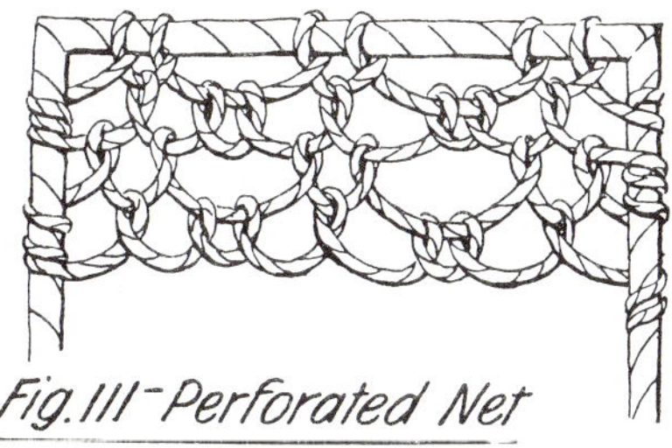

Fig. 111 - Perforated Net

variations by altering the stitches of which they are composed.

In making Needle Point, a protector is often used, to keep the
work from touching the hands unnecessarily.  This consists of
a piece of material to cover the work, with a round hole cut in it,
just large enough for the worker to get at the part she is making.

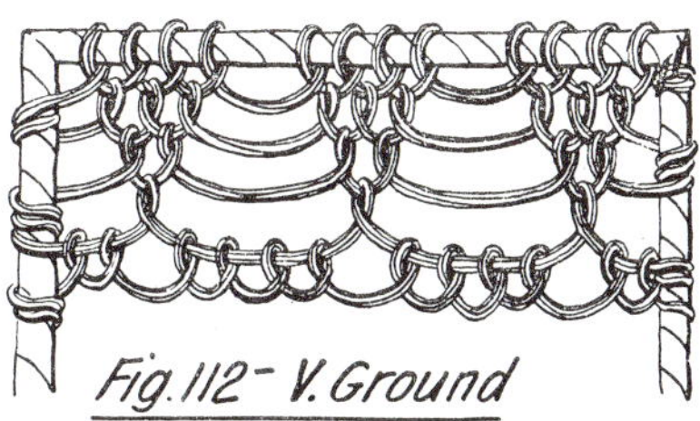

Fig. 112 - V. Ground

The material used should be smooth, pliable and one that can be
easily cleansed.

# CHAPTER XIII

# THE DEVELOPMENT OF HAND-MADE LACE

EVEN when the world was young and life very primitive, necessity must have been found for an equivalent to needle and thread, with which to attach skins one to another and fix them into convenient shapes.

Simple needles have been discovered among the relics of primeval man in many parts of the world, far distant from each other. These, for the most part, were made of bone; though some, in Scandinavian tumuli, where such traces of luxury might be little expected, were discovered that were fashioned from gold.

With advancing civilisation the use of the needle was extended from acts of need to works of ornamentation. Simple attempts took at first probably the form of even stitches placed at regular intervals, but expanded into embroidery of an elaborate kind as early as the times of ancient Egypt and primeval China.

In the earliest days of skin-clad humanity there must have been a need for snares, both for land animals and fish, which was doubtless soon supplied by some method of knotting or netting. There is evidence that nets of flax string were made by the ancient Egyptians by means of needles not unlike our own.

It is easy to imagine that, when people were able to make nets for necessary purposes with coarse materials, it would soon occur to those interested in the manufacture of articles for personal adornment, that by the use of a finer size of thread or more costly materials, such as silk or gold, a valuable adjunct would be found for their work. That this was actually the case we have evidence in the relics found in tombs as well as in ancient records.

From passages in Exodus it is evident that embroidery was used in the times of Moses, while in Isaiah we read of Egypt working in fine flax and network; though from the context it is probable that the nets were used for practical purposes. Later on, Ezekiel speaks plainly of both Syrian and Egyptian embroidery.

Here it is plain to see that we have the origin of lace, though it appears to have been long in taking final shape.

Most text-books are contented with tracing lace back to the Middle Ages, but Mlle Charles, O.A., and M. L. Pagés, in their interesting book, *Les Broderies et Les Dentelles*, go much further and mention that in the course of Egyptian excavations mummies have been found clothed in the costumes which they wore in life.  Certain of them have decorations for the hair, bags, purses, trimmings, and even tunics or jackets made of work which we can but attribute to the result of using some kind of bobbins. These are of different designs and stitches, but mostly of the class called Guipure, and may probably be the most ancient lacework in existence.

Mlle Charles further says that an old Chinese work was found in the French National Library with the representation of a machine, with which a woman was making a network similar to those made in the Egyptian tombs.  In the same book were also pictures of caps or bonnets similar to those worn by the mummies.

Our French authors also mention that in castles and convents in Europe the primitive rudiments of a bobbin lace have long been hidden, which had fallen into disuse before the present lace industry was touched.

The brilliant success of the Venetian needle lace from a commercial point of view may have inspired the idea of reviving the fabrication of this old bobbin lace ; though it may be that the latter was at the time a popular handiwork, and was actually displaced by the needle lace.  Whatever its origin, the development of bobbin lace did not wait long after the introduction of Venetian Point, but was soon able, in some measure, to imitate its patterns.

From very early times geometrical patterns were embroidered in coloured silks on a network of small square meshes in many parts of Europe.  In the 13th and 14th centuries this was known as " opus filatorium " and " opus araneum," or in English, " threadwork " and " spiderwork."  Examples dating from the 13th century may probably be seen in several public collections.

This work became known in Italy as " square net point," and in France as " lacis."  When darned the meshes and stitches were counted and from this it took the name of " point conté " beside its obvious designation of " darned netting."

It is difficult to define lace exactly, but it is probably correct to say that it is a decorative material, made of strands, which are twisted, stitched or plaited together, without being united with any substance already woven.

This definition excludes Carrickmacross, Limerick and Tambour, which are always recognised as laces, but these are really light and artistic embroideries.

Knitting, crochet, tatting, hairpin work and Tenerife are undoubtedly included among laces, crochet especially having developed in Ireland into an artistic industry of considerable importance under the name of Irish Point : but having had a separate development they may be left outside the present discussion.

Cutwork was evolved from the embroidery on net. On a light frame was fastened a network of threads with fine lawn fixed under it. The pattern was then embroidered along the threads to the lawn back and the superfluous lawn drawn or cut away.

From Drawn Threadwork (in which patterns were darned or stitched on threads left after the withdrawal of others) was evolved Reticella, and that Punto in Aria which seems likely to have been the mother of needle lace or may indeed be itself called the first attempt at Venetian Point : but Cutwork, in which rectangular spaces in linen were filled with button-holed threads and other stitches, appears to have its own ancestral claim. In fact it is impossible to apportion the influences which resulted in lace proper, either in Needle Point or Pillow.

Embroidery, drawn threadwork, spiderwork and cutwork led to Needle Point. Having been accustomed to make delicate and beautiful patterns by means of stitches on the net or linen threads, it occurred to certain workers to omit the foundation of net or linen, and to form their patterns of stitches alone, by the aid of threads fastened to a design in such a way as to form the outline of each flower or ornament.

Thus was formed the first needle-point lace, or as its makers first called it, to distinguish it from embroidery and drawnwork, " Point in the Air " : that is to say, a work formed by stitches, with no net or cloth foundation.

The workers were accustomed to the limitations of the net or drawn threads, hence their patterns were, at first, simple and geometrical : but with the coming of the Renaissance, when every known art took new life, their patterns became free and flowing or attempted bold figures, perhaps better planned than executed.

Where painting and its kindred arts were earliest established there lace also flourished, namely in Italy and Flanders, though, later on, painters have left records of lace in other countries.

One Dutch portrait of a date before 1684 has net ground lace upon it. In the English National Gallery is a portrait of James II, dated 1685, with cravat and cuffs of Needle Point : and of a date yet earlier, 1614, a picture of Mary Countess of Pembroke, wearing coif and cuffs of Reticella.

The origin of pillow lace has been much disputed, probably owing to the fact that some primitive bobbin work was very widely known and was stimulated by the introduction of Needle Point into a rapid and widespread development.

The Flemings have been largely accorded the honour of the

invention, but in regard to all lace there was the closest rivalry between them and the Italians.  It is known that the Flemish lace pattern-books of the 16th century have the same characteristics as those issued for the Venetians and Italians, and that, in Italy, the art of twisting and plaiting threads by means of bobbins was known and practised from an early period.

As regards France, Henry III of that country, who reigned from 1574 to 1589, appointed a Venetian as pattern-maker to his Court for needlework and lace, but evidently the industry did not naturalise to any extent, for we find edicts to check the wearing of foreign lace, by which so much money was taken out of the country.  This caused some indignation and a poem was written, entitled the " Revolt of the Laces," personifying the well-known varieties, which is useful as a record of those then made.  Abraham Bosse, an engraver, also depicts the sadness of a fashionable lady, dressed in linen collar and cuffs, stowing away clothing trimmed with beautiful lace.

Colbert, Minister of Louis XIV, worked out a more sensible plan and tried to keep the money at home by producing the lace in the country by the hands of French people.  In 1665 there was an edict to found lace-making centres at Alençon and other places.

Diplomacy was freely used, and intrigue perhaps not excluded, in obtaining Venetian lace workers as instructors at the centres. A subsidy was given of 36,000 francs, nearly £1500, and a company formed to organise the industry.

In Germany the peasants of the Harz Mountains were taught by Barbara Uttman to make simple laces, but with no great success.  German lace has never reached a position as a widespread industry.

The Roman Church and the Courts of Europe have always been the chief patrons of lace-making.  Most important Roman Catholic Churches have large stores of wonderful old lace of early and modern date.  In the 12th century, when the tomb of St Cuthbert was opened, embroidered net was found on one of his vestments, a very early date for work of that kind.

Mrs Pallisser quotes from a letter written by an English lady in 1771 a description of the ceremony in which the Pope washes the feet of twelve poor men, during which " one of his Cardinals brought him an apron of Old Point with a broad border of Mechlin lace and tied it with a broad ribbon round his Holiness' waist."

The lace department of the South Kensington Museum has many beautiful examples of Church lace.

In England, as on the Continent, some kind of bobbin work was known in very early days, for in a Harleian manuscript of the reigns of Henry VI and Edward IV there is an elaborate description of the ways of twisting and plaiting thread together, in twos, threes, fours, etc., up to tens and fifteens. Balls of thread stuck on the fingers were used instead of bobbins, and when broad plaits were made assistant persons provided extra hands.

Whether this work developed at home or whether bobbin lace-making was brought from abroad is difficult to decide, but it was probably the latter to some extent if not altogether. Tradition says that Katherine of Aragon, when living at Ampthill Park, taught the peasants near her to make the lace, which is still known by her name, a border with a net ground.

Towards the end of the reign of James I a custom arose of employing religious designs for lace, cutwork, etc., which suggested the lines given in a play by Jasper Mayne commencing :

> "She makes religious petticoats. For flowers
> She'll make Church Histories."

Beaumont and Fletcher, too, in their play, "The Custom of the Country," say :

> "Sure you should be
> Without a neat historical shirt."

Even in those days of long ago, modern extravagance was anticipated, for in the warrant for the marriage expenses of the Princess Elizabeth it says : "Lady Arabella [Stuart] though still in the Tower, has shown her joy by buying four new gowns, one of which cost £1500 in addition to gold cheine laze, silver spangled, silver looped, myllen bone lace, drawne-work pointe, black silk Naples lace," etc. Among other items came an entry of silver-bone lace.

For a ruff of the time of James I, 25 yards of lace were needed for edging, apart from the material for the ruff itself, which was likely to be of lace or cutwork.

In Queen Elizabeth's time lace was sometimes made of ladies' hair and called Point Tresse. Mary Queen of Scots is said to have received a present of some of this lace from Darnley's mother. It is said that grey hair made the most valuable lace of this description. Hence the line :

> "And Bedford's matrons wove their snowy locks."

The year 1801 was considered, by Mrs Pallisser, to be the culminating point of lace prosperity, and it was probably about this time that in England as well as in Flanders some men are said to have left their work on the land for the pillow-lace industry, which was found more profitable. One widow of eighty is supposed to have brought up seven children, besides supporting herself, on the proceeds of the sale of a narrow edging sold at 6d. per yard.

Early in the 18th century, after the visit of Peter the Great to

Paris, lace-making was patronised by the Russian Court, but only the coarser and simpler kinds have continued to be made.

No one knows the exact circumstances concerning Spanish lace. There was a kind called Spanish Point, which was really Veneian and was probably named for the place to which it was certainly largely exported. On the other hand, a little of this Spanish Point was probably made in Spanish convents. A white Guipure lace was made in Spain, also a blond lace, both in black and in white.

In the Scandinavian countries we know of little lace, properly so called, beyond the coarser kinds used for the trimming of towels, sheets, tablecloths, etc. In this, and in Russian lace, blue or red thread is frequently used for decoration. But a very beautiful embroidery is made there, in which lace stitches are inserted after the manner of the old cutwork.

The varieties of lace may be divided into two classes : Needle Point—the first, both in supposed date of invention and actual money value ; and Pillow or Bobbin Lace.

In point of beauty it is hard to judge between them, the Needle Point being generally richer in effect, while the Pillow Lace excels in a dainty lightness nearly akin to frost on a window-pane.

Bobbin Lace is formed by plaiting, weaving and twisting threads, which are kept in a set form by means of pins placed in prepared holes.

Needle Point is built up of button-hole stitches, simple or otherwise, with some twisted threads.

Traces are found of Needle Point in the 15th century. Reti-cella had a little of the appearance of crochet, but soon altered its style, took more flowing and graceful designs, and developed into that Venetian Point, which has had such a wide and well-merited reputation. This was largely made in the convents for Church purposes. One of its earliest varieties is the Flat Venetian Point, with conventional if not geometrical flowers and ornaments, held together by button-holed bars.

Many varieties of lace were made in Venice, but three have always been specially distinguished by its name. There is first the Flat Venetian in which the outlines to the lace and pattern were only slightly raised above the rest of the pattern.

The Raised or Grand Venetian had every outline accentuated by swelling and diminishing lines of threads, covered either by overcasting or a coat of some fine material. This is its cor-donnet.

The Rose Point had its cordonnet richly ornamented with loops, wheels and roses of button-holing, decorated with picots, until some specimens looked like carved ivory.

Coralline Point, a less known variety, is said to have been

made to imitate a branch of coral, the gift of the worker's sailor lover, and is very beautiful.

In France, about 1665, under the fostering care of Colbert, Mme Laperière was largely instrumental in starting the successful development of Point d'Alençon, a very beautiful lace of a style distinct from that of Venice. Towards 1717 its first ground of hexagonal bars gave place to the net, which was its characteristic feature. Argentan followed with a more open ground and from it Argentella was derived, with its striking ground of tiny webs.

The Brussels Point de Gaze was probably derived from Alençon rather than Venice. The speciality of Point de Gaze is its extreme lightness and delicacy, its cordonnet, unlike those of France and Italy, having no heavy covering of button-holing.

In the larger manufactories of Needle Point it is a common practice for the workers to specialise. The pattern is cut up and divided according to the skill of the worker. One will make the plainer parts of the flowers, another puts in the more ornamental centres. The various parts are fixed in position by another skilled worker, and yet others fill in the grounding.

The making of Bobbin Lace being carried on in so many widely separated places, even more varieties have been started in this than in the Needle Point. Like the latter, the finest and most artistic kinds are made in the two great Art Centres of Italy and Belgium, while Devon gives England an honourable place among the producers of fine lace.

Some quaint bobbin lace, with meandering straws in lieu of pattern, was formerly made in Italy, and lace entirely of straw is made in a small Swiss valley.

Outside Europe lace-making has been started in several countries. China has some interesting Filet Lace and in that country, India and Ceylon, missionary schools are giving instruction, principally for making simple laces.

As State-aid in England has never subsidised the industry or helped in the designing of artistic patterns, lace here could not be expected to attain the high artistic finish that has been reached on the Continent. Yet private enterprise has done much to improve both design and workmanship. The Arts and Crafts Exhibitions help in this, both encouraging workers and showing them each other's achievements.

English lace has its own special perfections. Its workmanship is sometimes marvellous and generally good ; the difference between it and the best Continental work being that between the work of a group of amateurs, some of whom are distinguished, and the output of a manufactory of good standing, whose work keeps an even standard of excellence.

England's best lace has generally come from Devon, Dorset and Bucks, while Bedford, Hunts and Nottingham have given a large output, though the production of the latter is now chiefly, if not entirely, machine made.

By the end of the 16th century narrow laces, such as those known as Lille, were worn both by citizens and country people as trimmings for their caps and dresses ; and by the early part of the next century it is said that this kind of lace was made in the Isle of France by more than ten thousand families.

The Lille type of lace has a plain net ground, with some simple design outlined with a thick thread. Its production was very widely distributed, but, in France, found its headquarters in the neighbourhood of Lille and in England in the Midlands, more especially in Buckinghamshire.

Mechlin is a very beautiful and valuable lace, which without careful observation might easily be mistaken for Lille. It is exceptionally fine, but strength is given by extra stitches at every mesh of the grounding, making it, naturally, expensive.

Valenciennes has what is called a double ground, made by plaiting four bobbins instead of twisting two, which makes it very strong even in its finer qualities.

Its centre of manufacture, after deserting the town from which it takes its name, established itself at Ypres and the lace is made in many parts of Belgium. Before the introduction of machine lace in that county it was made in Nottinghamshire.

Maltese, with its meandering paths of linenwork, its plaited bars and loops and characteristic leaves of basket stitch, is one of the most widely known laces that are made. Besides its original habitat, in the South of Europe, this lace has found a settled home in the English Midlands, more particularly in Bedfordshire. Until recent years its patterns were geometrical and not remarkable for beauty : but the revival of lace-making, which took place in England at the beginning of the present century, turned the attention of designers to the needs of Maltese. But there is still scope for artistic attention to this as well as to the finer laces.

Coarse Guipure laces, those with a pattern having a bar ground and Torchon, change gradually, the one into the other, and are perhaps the most widely distributed of all varieties. Naturally so, when we consider that their manufacture is simple and easy and so likely to appeal to a wide circle of workers. Though, for all this, it is an undoubted fact that finer and more difficult laces give far better return for the labour bestowed upon them.

It is useless to try to enumerate the localities where these simpler laces are made, they are too widely distributed.

Bruges is the name generally given to a lace in which the pattern is made before its ground of simple bars, and the thread is not of the finest. The Bruges people, who make it so largely, prefer to call it Brussels, or Duchesse, from which it differs in its coarser texture, and sometimes less perfect finish. It is an attractive lace, and one often made by amateurs, who like to get over their work quickly. Beside its name city it is made in Brussels, Ghent and other Belgian districts.

Some exquisitely fine bobbin lace of the Guipure or bar-ground order is made both in Italy and Belgium, as well as in some English centres.

Duchesse, which is the finest Belgian Guipure lace, and Honiton, which is also Guipure, and often very fine, have much in common. But the Belgian lace generally excels our own in design, and in a certain style of execution, which has come, no doubt, from traditional training. Still, for good workmanship and finish, it would be hard to surpass some of our fine English work.

Devon net-ground lace should not be confused with Honiton, though it often goes by that name. It has the higher value when the net is made with the needle, though some with the bobbin net ground is not far behind in beauty or worth.

The Brussels net-ground lace, though very strong, has a lighter appearance than the English and when its net is needle-made has something of the look of the Point de Gaze. Only a lace worker can appreciate the bold and dexterous methods employed by the Belgian expert. There has been much discussion as to why the Brussels net-ground lace, undoubtedly made in Belgium, should have been called " Point d'Angleterre," but, like the " Spanish Point," it was probably named for the country which bought it so largely, even in the days when the duty upon foreign lace was considerable. Smuggling was prevalent and the name English Point may have been found convenient.

The production of these laces in Belgium is more widespread than is generally supposed, the workers being scattered throughout the country in winter, but flocking into the towns in the tourist season, where, sitting in the open with their pillows, many a stray franc finds its way into their possession as purchase money or as a tip.

To some extent this is the case in Dorset and Devon. Wherever there is a professional lace-worker, a seat at the open door, or just outside it, seems to suggest itself as a suitable place for her industry.

Early in the present century new centres were started in Norfolk and in the vicinity of Cambridge, but for English people the lace is scarcely well enough paid to attract workers who have no inherited leaning to that way of earning their bread.

To those new to it, the making of bobbin lace is most interesting. Its attraction perhaps lies in its mixture of simplicity and mystery. Here are thread, pins, sticks, and a paper with pinholes in it attached to a cushion ; all very simple things.

But then there is such swift passings of these thread-covered sticks, such twisting and twirling and sticking of pins into pin-holes, that it is hard for a mere onlooker to imagine how a fragile and dainty fabric can result from all these apparently casual movements.

To the initiated the whole thing is very simple.   There is a suitable pillow with a pattern pinned upon it, on which every outline is perforated with pinholes.   There are bobbins, too, wound with thread.   The threads of some of the bobbins are suspended from pins and hang between the pinholes to form the warp threads of the tiny loom.   Other threads, on other bobbins, weave in and out, backwards and forwards, across the first and are fixed by twists and plaits around the pin, which is placed in that hole which fixes the line last worked into its position.   Quite simple and easy to learn step by step.   So easy is it, that in the old days, before School Boards, many little ones began to learn the lace at four years old.

Many of the relics of the old lace-making days are most interesting.   There are quaint wooden " Turns " with which to wind thread from skeins upon bobbins.   Many different kinds of Pillow Stands are to be found both in England and on the Continent.

Then there are queer glass globes or bottles, which were used in the days of tallow candles, when light was such a difficulty as only those can realise who have tried to make fine lace with insufficient illumination.   In the lace schools these bottles were filled with water and placed in such a position that the rays from a candle fell through them upon the worker's pillow, intensifying the light and clearing it of flickering shadows.

Handsome old oak chests are still in existence of which the upper or box part could be used for pillows, which every lace-worker loves to multiply, while underneath, a large drawer provided places for lace, bobbins, patterns and minor paraphernalia.

The old patterns and bobbins are, perhaps, the most interesting of these antique relics.

For the patterns for Maltese and Buckingham laces, which are worked backwards and forwards across a strip placed round the centre of the pillow, parchment or cardboard is found necessary, and in the old patterns the former was chiefly used.   This was because only the strongest materials could stand the constant wear when very many yards were made of each pattern, each worker often depending for her livelihood on the proceeds of one or two designs.

The Devon lace was different.   The change of pattern was more frequent, so that durability was not so essential.   Hence any handy piece of fairly strong paper was apt to be utilised, and patterns were frequently renewed.   As those who copied them were, frequently, neither skilful nor careful, many old patterns have lost their original forms and can only be restored by guess-work.

Pattern hunting in Devon leads to many surprises, but, such as they are, they are numerous enough.  One vendor stated some years back that she had inherited or otherwise acquired a mat-tress cover full of them.  Her prices, though, did not suggest this plethora.

As to bobbins : those of different countries and even districts differ widely from each other.  The general form is that of a short stick, on one end of which is a place for the winding of the thread, while the other is intended to be lifted between the fingers.  It is chiefly the latter end which differs and upon which decoration was so frequently lavished.  In England this end keeps much the form of a round stick, while on the Continent it is generally made into a knob, which gives weight to the bobbin.

Buckingham lace has a coarser thread (or gimp) to outline its patterns, and to distinguish this quickly from the other threads its workers wind them on stouter bobbins often weighted with pewter rings.  Some of the old wooden bobbins are very inter-esting, delicately carved, black with age and polished by much fingering.  Many old bobbins are made of brass, copper or pewter and are ornamented with beads and some even inlaid with turquoise.

Other antique bobbins are made of bone, some inlaid with brass wire, or pewter rings, while others are painted or stained with different colours.  Some have names upon them and others mottoes, such as : " Love the giver." " Marry me quick."  " I love you as birds love cress."  " Be constant and true to me, my dear."  " I long to wed the lad I love." " A present from my true love."  " Love me or leave me."

Another very distinct variety is called the " Church Window " or " Baby " bobbin, in which one, two or even three tiny bobbins are seen through small window-frames of Gothic shape.

In the Buckingham and Maltese lace it is of importance that the bobbins should be heavy enough to give a considerable ten-sion to the thread, and for this reason Midland workers generally weight their bobbins.  The recognised way of doing this is to bore a hole in the end of the bobbin furthest from the thread, to pass a piece of brass wire through it, and on the wire to string enough beads to give the desired strain.  Some old beads are quite valuable ; many Venetian may be found and some that have been sand-papered to a chequered square, which are also valued by collectors as well as workers.

The writer wishes to express her acknowledgments to Mrs Pallisser, Mr Alan Cole, and others, for information obtained from their works for this outline, the " Glossary " and " Lace Centres," also to the authorities of the South Kensington Museum for permission to reproduce the two photographs given as frontispiece and facing p. 121.

# LACES AND THEIR CENTRES

ALENÇON : Needle Point with net, introduced by Colbert to rival Venetian Point.

ALOE L. : Made from fibres of aloes.

ANTWERP : Potten Kant.  Edging with design of flower in pot.

ARGENTAN : French needle, lace fine button-holed ground.

ARGENTELLA : French needle lace with special ground developed from Argentan.

ASBESTOS : Made from fibres of Asbestos.

AUVERGNE : Guipure and other border laces.

AVE MARIA : A very narrow Dieppe pattern.

BABY L. : Narrow, with fine net for baby linen.

BATH BRUSSELS : Old name for Honiton.

BAYEUX : Chantilly.

BEDFORDSHIRE : Two laces, Maltese style and some net-ground edgings.

BEDS POINT : Regency Point.

BEGGAR'S L. : Torchon, Gueuse.  Very simple lace.

BINCHE : A fine bobbin lace.

BIZETTES : Bands of bobbin net (old).  A coarse peasant lace of the end of 15th century.

BLONDE : A silk lace.  Heavy pattern.  Fine ground.  Made in Northern France and Spain.

BRUGES : Laces of many kinds, especially a rather coarse make of Duchesse.

BRUSSELS : Lace of nearly every kind, especially Point de Gaze, Duchesse and fine pillow lace with net ground.

BUCKINGHAMSHIRE : A fine border lace with net ground and some Maltese.

BULLION : Made of gold or silver.

BURRANO : Grounded Venetian.

CADIZ : Guipure appliqué.

CAMPANE : Narrow bobbin lace of the end of 16th century.

CANAILLE : Renaissance lace.

CARNIVAL L. : Venetian Point.

CARRICKMACROSS : Fine linen appliquéd on net.  Irish.

CATERPILLAR L. : Made of rolled-out paste, the pattern on which is oiled and so left intact and the ground eaten by caterpillars.

CHANTILLY : A fine French lace with open net ground.
CLUNY : A Guipure border lace.
COLBERT : Point d'Alençon.
CORALLINE : A lovely Venetian needle lace, with coral-like pattern.
CORK L. : Irish crochet.
CRAPONNE : A Guipure lace.
CRETAN L. : Method doubtful.   Peculiar, geometrical.
CROWN L. : With patterns of crowns, 16th century.

DALECARLIAN : Lace of patterns 200 years old, worn by the
    peasants.
DARNED L. : Limerick.   Irish.   Net ground.
DENTELLE : Lace with net ground, such as Point de Gaze and
    Mechlin.
DENTELLE DE LA CHASSE : Lace with hunting figures.
    ,,        ,,   ,,   SORCIÈRE : Modern Mechlin lace.
    ,,        ,,   ,,   VIERGE : 18th century.   Double ground.
DEVONIAN L. : Flowers, etc., applied on Honiton ground.
DIEPPE : Resembling Valenciennes.
DORSETSHIRE : Formerly made very fine lace, Honiton style.
DRAWNWORK : Needlework on linen, with drawn threads.
DROCHELL : A Belgian bobbin net.
DUCHESSE : A fine Brussels Guipure lace.
DUTCH L. : Mostly strong.   Of good thread.

EN L'AIR, POINT D' : Ancient needle lace, derived from Point
    Coupé.
ESPAGNE, POINT DE : Venetian Point.

FALSE VALENCIENNES : A valuable old lace, made outside its
    name town.
FEDORA : Point appliqué.
FILET BRODÉ : Embroidered net.
FILET L. : Chinese square mesh.
FLANDERS : First, Needle Point, and later most kinds of bobbin
    lace.
FLAT POINT : Flat Venetian Needle Point.
FRANCE, POINT DE : Alençon.

GAZE, POINT DE : A light, modern Belgian needle lace.
GENOESE : Vandyked tape lace.   Guipure.
GRAMMONT : Formerly cheap, white thread.   Now black.
GROS POINT DE VENISE : Venetian Point.
GUEUSE : Beggar's lace.   Narrow bobbin lace of end of 16th
    century.   Torchon.
GUIPURE : Lace with bar or open ground, such as Venetian,
    Bruges or Maltese.

HAIR L. : Made of human hair.
HONITON : Devon Guipure lace, in which the pattern is made
before the ground.

IRLANDE, POINT D' : Needle Point, Venetian style.
IRISH POINT : Fine crochet lace.
IRISH ROSE POINT : A flat Needle Point.
ISLE OF WIGHT L. : A kind of Limerick.

JESUIT L. : Made of fine white flax or silk.

KNOTTED L. : Macramé.

LACIS : An ancient darned netting.
LILLE : A fine border lace in which pattern and net ground are
worked together.
LIMERICK : Luneville. Patterns run on net.
LUXEUIL : A Guipure lace.

MACRAME : A coarse knotted lace.
MADAGASCAR : Guipure lace.
MALTESE : A Guipure of linenwork paths and basketwork
leaves.
MANILLA L. : Made of grass in the Philippine Islands.
MARLY : A French bobbin net of 18th century.
MECHLIN : Malines and formerly Macklin. A valuable border
lace with ground of special net.
MIGNONETTE : A narrow bobbin lace of the end of 16th century.
MILANESE : A tape lace with net ground.
MIRECOURT : Chantilly, Guipure and other border laces.
MODENA : Square meshed lace.

NANDUTI L. : Made on cardboard in Paraguay of silk and thread.
NEIGE, POINT DE : Rose Point.
NORTHAMPTONSHIRE : Lace with fine net ground, like Bucks and
Beds.
NOTTINGHAMSHIRE : Machine lace. Formerly Tambour and
Valenciennes.

OYAH : Turkish crochet lace.

PASSEMENT : Lace dating before 1600.
PEASANT L. : Simple laces of Torchon style.
PLAITED L. : Point de Genes. Vandyked. Made with four
threads.
PLAUEN : A centre for machine lace.

POINT ALENCON : A French needle lace with net ground.
  ,,     ANGLETERRE : An old name for Brussels smuggled into England.
  ,,     APPLIQUÉ : Sprigs applied to machine net.
  ,,     ARGENTAN : A needle lace with ground of button-holed meshes.
  ,,     ARGENTELLA : A French needle lace made also at Abbisola in Italy. Developed from Argentan with Rosacé ground.
  ,,     BURANO : Grounded Venetian Point.
  ,,     CANAILLE : Renaissance, Guipure with tape, often machine made.
  ,,     COLBERT : Alençon.
  ,,     CORALLINE : Lovely old Venetian lace with pattern founded on coral.
  ,,     COUPÉ : An ancient work from which needle lace was developed.
  ,,     CRAPONNE : Guipure.
  ,,     EN L'AIR : Ancient needle lace with no linen foundation.
  ,,     ESPAGNE : Venetian Point.
  ,,     FLAT : Flat Venetian. Modern.
  ,,     FRANCE : Alençon.
  ,,     GAZE : A modern Belgian light needle lace.
  ,,     GENES FRISÉ : Plaited lace.
  ,,     IRLANDE : Needle lace, Venetian style.
  ,,     LUXEUIL : Guipure.
  ,,     MILAN : Guipure pillow lace.
  ,,     NEIGE : Rose Point.
  ,,     PLAT : Bobbin lace.
  ,,     POPE'S : Venetian Point.
  ,,     PUY : Chantilly.
  ,,     RAGUSE : Probably Venetian Point.
  ,,     ROSE : A rich and lovely Venetian needle lace.
  ,,     ROSE, IRISH : Modern flat Venetian Point.
  ,,     SEDAN : A beautiful needle lace with bold design.
  ,,     VENISE : Venetian Point.
POPE, POINT DE : Venetian Point.
POT L. : Antwerp lace.
POTTEN KANT : Antwerp lace. Design of flower in pot. Border lace.
PUY : Chantilly, Guipure and other laces.


RAGUSE : Probably Venetian Point.
RAPALLESE : Guipure of twists and plaits.
REGENCY POINT : A Guipure lace with smooth heading.
RENAISSANCE : A needle lace with machine-made braid. Also a style of Venetian Point.

RETICELLA : Ancient needlework from which needle lace developed.

ROSE POINT : Venetian Point with ornamental loops and picots.

RUSSIAN L. : Guipure with a bobbin-made tape.

SAXONY L. : A Guipure of twists and plaits.

SEAMING L. : An insertion for joining lace.

SEDAN L. : A beautiful needle lace of bold design.

SILVER L. : Made of silver thread.

SORCIÈRE, DENTELLE DE LA : A modern Mechlin lace.

SPANISH L. : Pillow Guipure, Blonde lace. Venetian Point sold to Spain.

SUFFOLK : Simple bobbin laces.

TAMBOUR L. : Worked on net in chain stitch.

TAPE GUIPURE L. : Bobbin tape in geometrical designs. Russian, etc.

TORCHON : A rather coarse lace of simple stitches.

TROLLY L. : Border lace.

VALENCIENNES : A border lace with plaited net. Now made in Belgium.

VALENCIENNES, FALSE : An old and valuable lace formerly made outside its name town.

VENETIAN POINT : A rich needle lace.

VENISE, GROS POINT DE : Raised Venetian Point.

VIERGE, DENTELLE DE LA : Pretty double ground border of 18th century.

WILTSHIRE : In the 17th and 18th centuries, made both needle and bobbin lace.

YAK : A woollen lace.

YPRES : Valenciennes.

# GLOSSARY

*A jours :* Ornamental stitches, to enrich special parts of lace.
 Fillings.
*Allover :* Lace of a width to cut for yokes, etc.
*Appliqué :* Separate patterns applied to net.
*Arraignée :* Spider. Cobweb.

*Bar, Needle :* Stitched or twisted strand to attach parts to each
  other.
 ,,  *Pillow :* Woven or twisted strand to attach parts to each
  other.
 ,,  *Feuille :* Worked in Reprise (basketwork).
 ,,  *Pearl-pin :* Stem stitch with picots.
 ,,  *Picots festonnés :* Button-holed, with button-holed picots.
 ,,  ,,   ,,  *doubles :* Button-holed, with the picots on
  both sides.
 ,,  *Snatch-pin :* With simple pinholes.
*Bead edge :* Simple pillow heading.
*Bertha or Berthe :* Lace for the shoulders or neck of a dinner or
 ball dress.
*Blind-pin :* A pin taken out and replaced in the same hole in the
 inner line of a curve.
*Bobbinet :* Bobbin-made net.
*Bobbin Lace :* Made with bobbins on a pillow.
*Bobbins :* Shaped sticks on which thread is wound for pillow
 lace-making.
*Bobbin-winders :* Machines for winding thread on bobbins.
*Bone Lace*
 ,,  *Point or*  } Old names for pillow lace.
 ,,  *Work*
*Border Lace :* Narrow lace.
*Boule de Neige :* An old net of little cobwebs.
*Bride's boucleés :* Button-holed bars.
 ,,  *écaillés :* Bar net.
 ,,  *Lace :* Guipure.
 ,,  *nez :* Bar net.
 ,,  *ornées*  } Bars with picots.
 ,,  *picotées*
*Buds :* Little rings.
*Button-hole stitch :* The principal stitch in needle lace.

*Cartisane :* Parchment or vellum, with pattern in silk or metal.
*Chain Lace :* Tambour.
   ,,   *stitch :* Crochet stitch.  In Tambour worked on net.
*Checked paper :* Paper ruled in small squares.
*Close a pin :* To make a stitch after setting a pin.  In bobbin lace.
*Close stitch (bobbin lace) :* Close work. Cloth stitch, Clothwork, Linen stitch, Whole stitch.
*Cloth, Covering :* Cloth to cover a pillow.
*Cloth stitch :* Two threads woven through two others.
*Clothwork :* A tissue-like fine linen, made by weaving threads. The usual materials of flower, etc., in pillow lace.
*Cord bobbins :* Bobbins left at the side, which make the cord of the open edge.
*Cordonnet :* A raised border to some Venetian Point. The Belgian outlining thread for pillow lace : thick, made of cotton.
*Corona :* " Raised work,'' which is made at the same time as the underlying flower or pattern.
*Coupé, Point :* Cutwork.  The origin of Needle Point.
*Couronnes :* In Raised Venetian.  Ornaments to the bordering Cordonnet.
*Covering-cloths :* Cloths for covering the pillow.
*Coxcombs :* Bars.  Old English.
*Crin, Fil de :* Outlining thread.  Cordonnet.
*Cucumber :* A Devon filling.
*Cutting off :* Tying and cutting off bobbins.
*Cutwork :* Ancient work from which Needle Point developed.
*Cutworks :* Devon basketwork fillings.

*Darning :* Limerick stitches.
*Doppel schlag :* Two half-stitches.
*Double ground :* Valenciennes.  Made with eight bobbins.
*Drawnwork :* Needlework on linen with drawn threads.
*Dressed pillow :* Pattern and covers arranged on a lace pillow.

*Edge, Bead :* A simple pillow lace heading.
   ,,   *Couple :* Cord bobbins.  Pair left at edge in Honiton, etc.
   ,,   *Pearl :* Edge with picots.
*Engrêlure :* Footing for sewing lace to other material.
*Entoilage, Point :* Much used in Needle Point.
*Escurial :* Footing (Mrs Pallisser).
*Eyelet hole :* A small hole with overcast margin.

*Fancy hole :* Devon name for pinhole-bordered hole in clothwork.
*Fedora :* Point Appliqué.
*Filet brodé :* Embroidered net.
*Filet Lace :* Made with square meshed net.

*Fil de Crin :* Cordonnet in pillow lace.
  „  „ *Trace :* Outlining thread or cord in needle lace.
*Fillings :* Ornamental work to enrich certain parts of lace.
*Flax :* Linen thread.
*Fleurs volants :* In Raised Venetian.  Ornaments the cordonnet
    of the body of the pattern.
*Fond :* Ground.  Net.
*Fond Chant :* Point de Paris.
*Footing*
*Footside* } The straight lower edge of lace.
*French Ground :* Point de Paris.  A six-point star net.
*Front :* The part of the pillow facing the worker.


*Gaining on a pin :* Changing the bobbins which have worked
    across (in Honiton lace), without putting in a pin.
*Ganz schlag :* Whole stitch.
*Gimp :* In the Midlands, thick linen thread for outlining the
    pattern.
*Gingles :* Beads on wire to weight and ornament bobbins.  Mid-
    lands.
*Gold Lace :* Made with gold thread.
*Grille :* Half-stitch, an open, net-like cloth.
*Groppo :* A knot or tie.
*Ground :* Net or bars, by which the pattern is held in place.
  „    *Double :* Valenciennes.  Plaited.
  „    *French* }
  „    *Wire* } Point de Paris.
*Guimpe :* Raised work in linen stitch.  Devon.
*Guipure :* Lace with bar or open, ground such as Venetian,
    Bruges, Maltese.
*Gymp :* Gimp.


*Hair-pin stitch :* Point de Paris.  Kat stitch.
*Half-stitch :* An openwork stitch like net.
  „ *-down :* Strips of pattern for Bucks lace.
*Hanging on :* Arranging bobbins on pins to commence lace.
*Heading*
*Head-side* } The upper edge of border laces.
*Hole, Eyelet :* A small hole overcast round its margin.
*Horse :* A stand for a lace pillow.


*Insertion :* A lace with straight heading.


*Jours, A :* Fillings.  Elaborate work for small spaces in Honiton
    and Brussels, etc.


*Kante :* Edge.

*Kat stitch* ⎫
*Kattern* ,, ⎬ Katten or Kattern, from Katherine of Aragon.
*Katten* ,, ⎭   Point de Paris.
*Klüppel Kissen :* Lace pillow.

*Lacetta :* Sheets of lace-like material taken from the lace bark-tree of Jamaica.
*Lappet :* Lace with two headings and shaped ends.
*Lead works :* Leaves in reprise (basketwork).
*Leaf stitch :* Basketwork used largely in Maltese.
*Leaf-stitch pin :* One with head bent round to support a thread.
*Legs :* " Straps " or bars.
*Linen stitch :* Cloth or whole stitch. Four threads woven together.
*Looping the bobbin :* Arranging the thread to stay at one length.
*Lozenge :* A " motif " in Tenerife lace.

*Maglia :* Mesh.
*Macklin* ⎫ Mechlin.
*Malines* ⎭
*Mat or Matt :* The closework of flowers and ornaments.
*Medallion :* A " motif " in Teneriffe lace.
*Medici collars :* Point de Venise supported by metal bars.
*Merletti a piombino :* Bobbin lace.
*Merletto :* Lace.
*Mezzo Punto :* Tape lace with Needle Point bars.
*Mitre :* A scallop.
*Modeno :* Laces with square mesh.
*Modes :* Fillings.
*Motif :* Sprig. A detachable piece of the pattern in Honiton, Brussels, etc.
*Mouches :* Spots worked on net.
*Moucheté Réseau :* Net with spots in Point Esprit.
*Mushroom pillow :* A rather flat round pillow for Honiton, Bruges, etc.

*Needle-pin :* A needle set in a handle.
  ,,   *Point :* A needle lace made chiefly of button-hole stitches.
  ,,   *Wigmaker's :* A tractor for making " sewings," being a fine hook on a curved wire.
*Neige, Point de :* Rose Point.
*Net :* A mesh ground to unite parts of lace.
*Noue, Point de :* Button-hole stitch.

*Œil de Perdrix :* Partridge eye, an ornamental ground in Mechlin.
*Open Lace :* Lace with no ground.
*Opus araneum :* Spider-work. Darned netting.
  ,,   *filatorium :* Thread-work. Darned netting.
*Ornées, Bride's :* Needle bars with picots.

*Passement :* Lace dating about 1600.
*Passementiers :* A Corporation with a monopoly for making passement, 1663.
*Passive :* A bobbin carrying a warp thread.
*Pearl or Purl :* Picot.  Loop.
  ,,   *edge :* Machine-made edge of loops, to sew on Limerick or Renaissance.
  ,,   *pin :* Devon name for picot.
  ,,   ,,   *bars :* Bars with picots.
*Pearling or Pearlin' :* Scotch lace.
*Perdrix, Œil de :* A Mechlin ground.
*Picot :* A loop.  Also a steel instrument for arranging the set of flowers, etc., in Point Alençon.
  ,,   *Bride's :* Bars with loops.
  ,,   *Festonnes :* Button-holed loops.
*Pillow :* A cushion on which bobbin lace is made.
*Pillow Lace :* Lace worked on a pillow with bobbins.
  ,,   *Mushroom :* Flat pillow for Bruges, etc.
*Pin, Blind :* A pin taken out and replaced in the same hole.
  ,,   *Gaining on a :* To exchange weavers without making an edge.
  ,,   *Winkie :* Edge with no cord bobbins.
*Pin-work :* Dutch name for lace.
*Piombino :* A small lead bobbin.
*Piqué knots :* Stitches in drawn threadwork.
*Plain hole :* Devon name for unbordered hole made in cloth-work.
*Plain-work :* Clothwork, whole stitch.
*Ply :* A single untwisted thread.
*Point :* A stitch.  A kind of lace using a certain stitch.
  ,,   *Brussels :* A strong fine and beautiful net.
  ,,   *Esprit :* Leaf stitch, basket stitch.
  ,,   *Genoa :* Basket stitch over two or four threads.
  ,,   *Racroc :* A stitch to join net grounds.
  ,,   *Rucroe :* A stitch of Calvados, Ireland, used to join flowers and scrolls.
  ,,   *Tresse :* Lace made of human hair.
*Powdered :* Dotted with small spots or sprigs.
*Pricker :* Needle-pin.  Instrument to make holes in patterns.
*Prickings :* Patterns.
*Punto :* Stitch.
*Punti :* Stitches.
*Punto in Aria :* Stitches in the air.  Early needle lace, with no linen foundation.
*Punto tirato :* Drawn threadwork.
*Purlings :* Devon for bars with picots.
*Putting back :* In Bucks, or Beds, lace, removing lace and pins from the end of a pattern to its commencement.

*Racroc :* A stitch for joining net grounds.

*Raised work :* An ornamental bar on clothwork in Honiton and Brussels, increasing its value.

*Real Lace :* Not machine-made nor imitating that of other sources.

*Réseau :* Net.

,, *avec bobine :* bobbin-made net.

,, *moucheté :* Net with Point Esprit spots.

,, *Rosacé :* Special net in Argentella lace.

,, *Vraie :* Needle or bobbin net. Not machine.

*Resting bobbins* ⎱
,, *weavers* ⎰ The cord-making pair left at the side.

*Reseuil* ⎱
*Rezie* ⎰ Réseau.

*Rings, Thread :* Used in Renaissance Point.

*Rolled work :* A raised work with twisted threads.

*Rucroe :* A stitch of Calvados, Ireland, used to join flowers and scrolls.

*Runners :* Workers, weavers. The pair of bobbins which go back and forth across clothwork in pillow lace.


*Sam Cloth :* Sampler.

*Seaming Lace :* Insertion for joining lace.

*Semés :* Powdering of spots, sprigs, etc.

*Sewing :* Uniting two parts of lace with a loop of thread.

*Shiny thread :* Devon name for linen thread used for outlining. Gimp.

*Signs, Devon :* 2 *pinholes :* Half-stitch.

    1  ,,   : Crossed gimps. Or hole.

    2  ,,  *above and* ⎱
    1  ,,  *below* ⎰ Pearl edge.

*Skip :* Small skein. Devon.

*Slip :* Small skein. Bucks.

*Snatch-pin bars :* Bars with simple pinholes. Devon.

*Sprig :* A complete flower or ornament in Honiton, Brussels, etc.

*Square Net Point :* Lacis, Point Conté. Darned netting.

*Sticks :* Bobbins.

*Stitch :* In pillow lace, two threads woven through two others.

,, *Button-hole :* The chief stitch of needle lace.

,, *Chain :* Crochet.

,, *Close :* Cloth, Linen and Whole stitch.

,, *Cloth :* In pillow lace, two threads woven through two others.

,, *Darning :* Stitch in Limerick.

,, *Hair-pin :* Point de Paris. Wire ground. Kat stitch.

,, *Half- :* An open, netlike stitch of three movements.

,, *Pearl :* Picot.

*Stitch, Stem* ⎫
 „ *Turning* ⎬ A half- and a whole-stitch.
 „ *Whole :* Cloth, Linen and Close stitch.

*Taking a Sewing :* Uniting two parts of lace with a loop of thread.
*Tallies :* Sticks, on which notches were cut to keep accounts.
*Tambour :* Lace made by chain stitches on net.
*Tap :* A section of a leaf.
*Tape, Chinese :* A tape made in China, a kind of bobbins.
 „ *Guipure :* Russian style, geometrical design.
*Ten-stick :* Devon name for guimpe, or raised work.
*Tie :* Bar.
*Toilé :* The close work of flowers, etc.
*Tombolo :* Lace pillow.
*Turn :* Bobbin winder.
*Turning stitch :* A half- and a whole-stitch.
*Turning the pillow :* Twisting it back to front.
*Turn-pins :* Loops on bars of Maltese lace.
*Turn side :* Head side.
*Trace, Filde :* In needle lace ; the thread outlining the pattern.
*Tractor :* A wigmaker's needle for " sewings."
*Trolle Kant* ⎫
*Trolly Lace* ⎬ Border lace.
*Trimming :* Neither an edging nor insertion.
*Trou-trou :* A pattern with perforations for threading ribbons.
*Tying off or out :* Fastening and cutting off bobbins.
*Trina :* Lace.
*Trine ad ago :* Needle lace.
*Trine a fuselli :* Bobbin-made lace.

*Vrai Réseau :* Real net. Hand-made. Not machine.

*Warp :* A thread running lengthwise in a tape, etc.
*Weaver :* A thread working through warps.
*Whole stitch :* Two threads worked through two others. Cloth
 or Linen stitch.
*Wigmaker's needle :* A tractor. Fine hook on a curved wire, for
 " sewings."
*Winkie-pin :* From the Dutch, Wincken, to be quick. Edge
 without cord bobbins.
*Wire ground :* Point de Paris.
*Woof :* A thread running across a tape, etc.
*Worker :* A weaver. A bobbin working through warps.

## Fig. 113

| | I. | II. | III. | IV. | V. | VI | VII. |
|---|---|---|---|---|---|---|---|
| Date...................... | 1540 to 1590. | 1590 to 1630. | 1620 to 1650. | 1650 to 1720. | 1720 to 1780. | 1790 to 1851. | 1851 to 1881. |
| Style of Pattern ... | Geometrical forms as worked in Reticella and Punt in aria. No "bride" or meshed ground used. | Introduction of floral and human forms, and slender scrolls, held together by "brides" or tyes. | Development of scrolls, and elaboration of details in scroll patterns. Commencement of use of meshed grounds. | Arrangements of detached ornamental details. More naturalistic imitation of flowers and pictorial representation of figures and portraits, and considerable use of ground of small meshes. | Designs composed of small details sprinkled over meshed grounds, and perpetuation of preceding patterns of 1690 to 1720. Use of machine made net commenced about 1720. | Perpetuation of some few traditional patterns, and mixture of conventional and naturalistic details. Repetition of motives. Loss of freshness in design. | Production of designs especially considered in regard to their reproduction in machine laces. Revival of old patterns. Mixture of all preceding styles. |
| Needle-point Lace ... | | | | | | | |
| Pillow-made Lace...... | | | | | | | |
| Machine-made Lace ... | | | | | | | |

*Table of the development of Lace, 1540-1881, by Mr Alan S. Cole, C.B.*

# BIBLIOGRAPHY

Some of the chief works on Lace published within the last hundred years in the United Kingdom and on the Continent of Europe.

*N.B.—Mere Catalogues of Lace at Exhibitions are not included.*

*Note.—All books are 8vo size and illustrated unless otherwise indicated. Those marked o.p. are out of print, and can only be obtained, if at all, second hand. Foreign books of the D.M.C. firm, Libraire Juven, etc., can be obtained from E. P. Rose Ltd., of Bedford. The prices for these books are approximately given.*

## ENGLISH

| Author. | Title. | Date. | Pages. | Price. | | Publisher. | Remarks. | Format. | Size. |
|---|---|---|---|---|---|---|---|---|---|
| Carita | *Lacis, practical instruction in* | 1909 | 143 | 10/6 | | Sampson Low | Instructive | 4to | 10 × 8 |
| ,, | ,, *diagrams for working* (3 sets) | 1910 | ... | 38/6 | | Do. | Useful | 4to | 10 × 8 |
| Caulfield, S. F. A., and Saward, B. C. | *Dictionary of Needlework* | 1882 | 528 | 21/- | o.p. | Upcott Gill | Most useful | l. 4to | 11 × 9 |
| Carnes, A. A. | *Bedfordshire Hand-made Lace* | 1913 | 16 | 6d. | o.p. | Local | Local pamphlet | oblong | ... |
| Channer, C. C., and Roberts | *Lace in the Midlands* | 1900 | 80 | 3/6 | | Methuen | Historical | ... | 7½ × 5 |
| Cole, Alan S. | *Cantor Lectures* (4) | 1881 | 39 | 1/- | o.p. | Society of Arts | Useful | ... | 9½ × 6½ |
| ,, | *Dublin ,, (2)* | 1884 | 20 | 1/- | o.p. | Dublin Museum | Pamphlet | ... | ... |
| ,, | *Hand-made Laces in the S.K.M.* | 1890 | ... | 42/- | o.p. | Sutton & Co. | Luxe, 30 plates | l. fol. | 18½ × 12½ |
| ,, (for Arundel Society) | *Anc. Needle Point and Pillow Lace* | 1875 | 30 | ... | o.p. | Arundel Society | Luxe, 20 plates | fol. | 16 × 12½ |
| ,, and Mrs Palliser | *Catalogue of Lace* | 1880 | 64 | 2/- | o.p. | S.K.M. | Official | ... | 7½ × 5 |
| ,, (in *Encyc. Brit.*) | *Lace* | ... | ... | ... | | ... | For reference | 4to | ... |
| Dillmont, Thérèse de | *Encyclopædia of Needlework* | 1891 | 750 | 3/6 | | D. M. C. Mulhouse | Invaluable. In 4 languages | {16mo and 8vo} | 5½ × 3½ |
| ,, | *Irish Crochet Lace* | 1912 | 64 | 2/6 | | ,, | ,, | oblong | 11½ × 8 |
| ,, | *Embroidery on Tulle* | 1909 | 40 | 1/6 | | ,, | ,, | ,, | ,, |
| ,, | *Needle-made Laces* | 1910 | 50 | 1/6 | | ,, | ,, | ,, | ,, |
| Eberlaine, H. D., and M'Clure, A. (Bainbridge, M. F.) | *Ch. XV. Practical Book of American Arts and Crafts* | 1916 | 36 | 30/- | | Lippincott | Historical | l. 8vo | 9 × 7 |
| Felkin, W. | *History of Lace Manufactures* | 1867 | ... | ... | o.p. | Local | Historical | ... | 7½ × 5 |
| Field, M. A. | *Australian Lace Crochet* | 1909 | 107 | 4/- | o.p. | Simpkin | Interesting | 4to | 10 × 7½ |
| Goldenberg, S. L. | *Lace : Its origin and history* | 1904 | 77 | ... | | Brentano, N.Y. | Historical | 4to | 10 × 7½ |
| Hawkins, D. W. | *Old Point Lace* | 1878 | 21 | 2/6 | o.p. | Chatto & Windus | 17 Examples | ... | 7½ × 5 |
| Head, R. E. | *Lace and Embroidery Collector* | 1921 | 252 | 7/6 | | Jenkins | Appendix, valuable, 19 plates | ... | 8 × 5½ |
| Jackson, Mrs Neville and Jesuran, E. | *History of Hand-made Lace* | 1900 | 245 | 31/6 | o.p. | Upcott Gill | A standard work. 19 plates | 4to | 10 × 9 |
| Jourdain, M. | *Old Lace* | 1905 | 121 | 42/- | o.p. | Batsford | Historical, 95 plates | 4to | 9 × 7 |
| Kellogg, Charlotte | *Robbins of Belgium* | 1920 | 314 | 8/6 | | Funk & Wagnalls | Anecdotal | ... | 8 × 5½ |

| Author. | Title. | Date. | Pages. | Price. | | Publisher. | Remarks. | Format. | Size. |
|---|---|---|---|---|---|---|---|---|---|
| Klickman, Flora | *Pillow Lace and Hand-worked Trimmings* | 1920 | 114 | 2/- | | Girls' Own Paper | Instructive | ... | 9 × 5½ |
| Lefèbure, A. (tr. Cole) | *Embroidery and Lace* | 1888 | 326 | ... | O.P. | Grevel | Historical | ... | 8 × 6 |
| Lefèbure, E. (tr. Johnston) | *Les Points de France* | 1912 | 103 | ... | O.P. | *New York* | Descriptive | ... | 10½ × 7½ |
| Lindsey, B. | *Irish Lace* | 1886 | 33 | 2/- | O.P. | Hodges of Dublin | Map of L. centres | ... | 7½ × 5 |
| Lowes, E. L. | *Chats on Lace* | 1908 | 210 | 9/- | | Fisher Unwin | Interesting | ... | 8 × 6 |
| Meredith, L. A. | *The Lacemakers* | 1865 | 375 | 6/- | O.P. | Jackson & Hodder | Irish, historical | ... | 8 × 5 |
| Millrow, M. E. W. | *Home Lace-making* | 1904 | 64 | 2/6 | | Scott, Greenwood & Co. | No illustrations | ... | 7½ × 5 |
| | *Church Lace* | 1920 | 124 | 6/- | | Do. | Useful designs | ... | 7½ × 5 |
| Mincoff, E., and Marriage, M. S. | *Pillow Lace* | 1907 | 231 | 18/- | | Murray | Useful | ... | 8 × 6 |
| Moody, A. P. | *Devon Lace Industry* | 1907 | 160 | 5/- | O.P. | Cassell | Historical | ... | 8 × 5 |
| ,, | *Lace Making and Collecting* | 1909 | 111 | 1/- | O.P. | Do. | Instructive | ... | 7 × 5 |
| Moore, N. H. | *The Lace Book* | 1908 | 206 | ... | O.P. | Hodder & Stoughton | Luxe, border on each page | ... | 11½ × 8½ |
| Muntz, E. (tr. Davis, L. J.) | *Tapisseries, etc.* | 1890 | ... | 5/- | O.P. | Cassell | ... | ... | 8 × 5 |
| Palliser, Mrs E. B. (Jourdain and Dryden) | *History of Lace* | 1902 | 536 | 52/6 | | Sampson Low | Luxe, a standard book | ... | 10 × 7 |
| Pollen, J. H. (intro. Cole) | *Seven Centuries of Lace* | 1908 | 60 | 30/- | O.P. | Heinemann | Luxe, useful | ... | 13 × 10 |
| Queen Newspaper | *Queen Lace Book* | 1874 | 40 | 5/- | O.P. | Q. Newspaper | Useful | 4to | 9 × 9 |
| Riego | *Modern Irish, Orris and Sequin Lace, 3 parts* | 1885 | 24 | 2/- | O.P. | Simpkin | ... | oblong | 5 × 9 |
| Ricci | *Old Italian Lace, 2 vols.* | 1913 | {278}{427} | 126/- | O.P. | Heinemann | Luxe | ... | 14½ × 11 |
| Sharp, M. (A. M. S.) | *Point and Pillow Lace* | 1899 | 202 | 9/- | | Murray | | ... | 8 × 6 |
| Sime, A. M. | *Pt. II. Torchon Lace Work* | 1909 | 153 | 2/6 | | Rose, *Bedford* | Useful | ... | 8 × 5 |
| Sylvia | *Macramé Lace* | 1885 | 5 | 1/- | O.P. | Ward Lock | | ... | 7 × 5 |
| Tebbs, L. A. | *The New Lace Embroidery* | 1905 | 49 | 11/- | | Chapman & Hall | | ... | 9 × 7 |
| ,, and R. | *Art of Bobbin Lace, 2 vols.* | 1907 | 82 | 8/6 | | Do. | | ... | 9 × 7 |
| Thomson, Ella | *Lace : How to judge and buy* | 1920 | 47 | 2/- | | Grafton | No illustrations, useful | ... | 7 × 4½ |
| Treadwin, Mrs | *Antique Point and Honiton Lace* | 1874 | 71 | ... | O.P. | Ward Lock | | ... | 9 × 7 |
| Weldon | *Nos.* 115, 124, 129, 153, 200, 213, 239 | ... | ... | 3d. each | | Weldon's Practical Needlework | | ... | ... |
| Whiting, G. | *A Lace Guide* | 1920 | 415 | ... | | Dutton | | ... | 10½ × 7½ |
| Wilkinson, M. E. | *Point Lace* | 1907 | 45 | 4/6 | | Scott, Greenwood & Co. | Instructive | oblong | 12 × 9 |
| Winser, Margaret and Aileen | *Elementary Practical Lace-making* | 1913 | 69 | ... | | Arnold, *Leeds* | Instructive | ... | 10 × 7½ |
| Wright, Thos. | *Romance of the Lace Pillow* | 1919 | 180 | ... | | Armstrong, *Olney* | Anecdotal | ... | 8½ × 5½ |

# FOREIGN

| Author. | Title. | Date. | Pages. | Place. | Price. | Size. | Format. | Remarks. |
|---|---|---|---|---|---|---|---|---|
| Bayard, Emile. | *L'Art de reconnaître les Dentelles* | 1914 | 345 | Paris | ... | $7\frac{1}{2} \times 5$ | ... | Valuable recipes and index |
| Brieuvres, M. de (Berry) | *La Dentelle, Histoire de la* | 1920 | 180 | ,, | .. | $8 \times 5\frac{1}{2}$ | ... | ... |
| Carlier, A. | *La Belgique dentellière* | 1898 | 118 | Brussels | ... | $10 \times 7$ | ... | ... |
| ,, | *Les Valenciennes* | 1902 | 66 | ,, | ... | $9\frac{1}{2} \times 6\frac{1}{2}$ | ... | Instructive |
| ,, de Lants heere | *Les Dentelles à la main* | 1906 | 40 | ,, | ... | $16 \times 12$ | ... | Luxe |
| Champeaux, M. A. | *Les Arts du Tissu* | 1893 | 144 | Paris | ... | $10\frac{1}{2} \times 7\frac{1}{2}$ | ... | Luxe au album |
| Charles, Mr Pagès L. | *Dentelles Françaises et Etrangères (2 vols.)* | 1907 | 480 | ,, | 3/6 | $11 \times 7\frac{1}{2}$ | ... | 40 Lessons |
| Despierres, G.. | *Histoire du Point D'Alençon (2 vols.)* | 1886 | 273 | ,, | 3/6 | $10 \times 6\frac{1}{2}$ | ... | ... |
| Davydoff, Sophie | *La Dentelle Russe* | 1895 | 28 | Leipzig | ... | $16 \times 12\frac{1}{2}$ | ... | Luxe, 80 plates |
| Dillmont, Thérèse de | *Les Dentelles aux Fuseaux* | 1921 | 192 | Mulhouse | 4/- | $10\frac{1}{2} \times 7$ | ... | Useful |
| ,, | *La Dentelle Renaissance* | 1915 | 76 | ,, | 2/6 | $10\frac{1}{2} \times 7$ | ... | Useful |
| Doumert, A. | *La Dentelle* | 1889 | 143 | Paris | ... | $8 \times 5$ | ... | Historical and Definitions |
| Dreger, Dr Moriz | *Geschichte der Spitz* | 1901 | 162 | Vienna | ... | $10\frac{1}{2} \times 8$ | ... | Historical |
| ,, | *Entwicklungsgeschichte der Spitze* | 1910 | 100 | ,, | ... | $10\frac{1}{2} \times 8$ | ... | No index |
| Frauberger, Tina | *Handbuch der Spitz Abenkunde* | 1894 | 272 | Leipzig | ... | $9 \times 6$ | ... | Instructive |
| Greef, G. de | *Louvrière Dentellière en Belgique* | 1886 | 127 | Brussels | ... | $5\frac{1}{2} \times 4$ | 4to | No illustrations |
| Hénon, H. | *L'Industrie des Tulles et Dentelles, 1815-1900* | 1902 | 600 | Paris | ... | ... | ... | ... |
| Haguet, Y. Crexells | *Historica y Técnica del Encage* | 1915 | 238 | Madrid | ... | $8 \times 5$ | ... | ... |
| Ilg, Albert | *Geschichte und Terminologie der alten Spitze* | 1901 | 71 | Vienna | ... | $9\frac{1}{2} \times 6$ | ... | ... |
| ,, | *Spitzen Alban* | 1876 | 64 | ,, | ... | $12 \times 9\frac{1}{2}$ | ... | 30 plates |
| Laprade, L. de | *Le Poinct de France* | 1905 | 396 | Paris | ... | $8 \times 6$ | ... | ... |
| Lefèbure, A. | *Dentelles et Guipures A. et M.* | 1904 | 314 | ,, | ... | $9 \times 5\frac{1}{2}$ | ... | ... |
| Melani, A. | *Svaghi Artistica Femmineli* | 1892 | 348 | Milan | ... | $10\frac{1}{2} \times 7\frac{1}{2}$ | ... | ... |
| Muntz, E. | *Tapisseries et Dentelles* | 1890 | 43 | Paris | ... | $12\frac{1}{2} \times 9\frac{1}{2}$ | ... | Luxe, 96 plates |
| Overloop, E. van | *Catalogue des ouvrages de la Dentelle* | 1906 | 433 | Brussels | ... | $10 \times 6$ | ... | No illustrations |
| ,, | *Matériaux pour servi a l'histoire de la Dentelle* | 1914 | 130 | ,, | ... | $17\frac{1}{2} \times 12\frac{1}{2}$ | ... | Luxe |
| Poupet, B. J. | *La Dentelle d'Alençon* | 1913 | 165 | Paris | ... | $10 \times 6\frac{1}{2}$ | ... | No illustrations |
| Ricci, Elisa | *Antiche Trine Italiane* | 1916 | 140 | Bergamo | ... | $14 \times 10\frac{1}{2}$ | fol. | Luxe, useful |
| Romanelli-Marone, G. | *La Trine a Fuselli in Italia* | 1902 | 331 | Milan | ... | $6 \times 4$ | ... | Useful |
| Sequin, J. | *La Dentelle* | 1875 | ... | Paris | ... | $16 \times 11\frac{1}{2}$ | ... | Luxe, Historical and Descriptive |
| 'Urbani de Gheltof, G. H. | *Les Arts Industriels a Venise* | 1885 | 300 | Vienna | ... | $10 \times 6\frac{1}{2}$ | ... | ... |
| ,, ,, | *I. Merletti a Venezia* | 1876 | 62 | ,, | ... | $8\frac{1}{2} \times 6$ | ... | No illustrations |
| Verhaegen, Pierre | *La Dentelle et la Broderie* | 1902 | 600 | Brussels | ... | $10\frac{1}{2} \times 7$ | ... | Luxe, official |
| ,, | *La Dentelle Belgique* | 1912 | 300 | ,, | 3/6 | $10\frac{1}{2} \times 7$ | ... | Historical |

# INDEX

PRINTED IN GREAT BRITAIN BY
THE EDINBURGH PRESS, 9 AND 11 YOUNG STREET, EDINBURGH.